T0178919

Insights You Need from
**Harvard
Business
Review**

# THE YEAR IN
# TECH 2024

# Insights You Need from Harvard Business Review

**Business is changing. Will you adapt or be left behind?**

Get up to speed and deepen your understanding of the topics that are shaping your company's future with the **Insights You Need from Harvard Business Review** series. Featuring HBR's smartest thinking on fast-moving issues—blockchain, cybersecurity, AI, and more—each book provides the foundation introduction and practical case studies your organization needs to compete today and collects the best research, interviews, and analysis to get it ready for tomorrow.

You can't afford to ignore how these issues will transform the landscape of business and society. The Insights You Need series will help you grasp these critical ideas—and prepare you and your company for the future.

## Books in the series include:

*Agile*

*Artificial Intelligence*

*Blockchain*

*Climate Change*

*Coronavirus: Leadership and Recovery*

*Crypto*

*Customer Data and Privacy*

*Cybersecurity*

*The Future of Work*

*Global Recession*

*Hybrid Workplace*

*Monopolies and Tech Giants*

*Multigenerational Workplace*

*Racial Justice*

*Strategic Analytics*

*Supply Chain*

*Web3*

*The Year in Tech, 2023*

*The Year in Tech, 2024*

Insights You Need from
**Harvard
Business
Review**

# THE YEAR IN
# TECH 2024

Harvard Business Review Press
Boston, Massachusetts

Copyright 2024 Harvard Business School Publishing Corporation
All rights reserved
Printed in the United States of America

10 9 8 7 6 5 4

The web addresses referenced in this book were live and correct at the time of the book's publication but may be subject to change.

Library of Congress Cataloging-in-Publication data is forthcoming.

ISBN: 978-1-64782-601-7
eISBN: 978-1-64782-602-4

The paper used in this publication meets the requirements of the American National Standard for Permanence of Paper for Publications and Documents in Libraries and Archives Z39.48-1992

# Contents

Contents

# Introduction

# INTEGRATIVE TECHNOLOGIES ARE THE NEW BUSINESS REALITY

by David De Cremer

Businesses that don't embrace emerging digital technologies are walking a path toward obsolescence. This book is a testimony to this fact. In the following pages, you will read about how new technologies such as brain sensors, generative AI, robotics, AR, and the metaverse are creating value in different functions such as HR, supply chains, customer service, and sales, as well as industries such as air travel and space exploration. As you read, you'll find out more about key trends, with lessons and practical takeaways to help your business along its digital transformation journey.

Interestingly, many of the technologies explored in this book are not truly "disruptive" innovations. In previous industrial revolutions—such as those that brought steam engines, numerical control, and the internet into mainstream use—the key technologies involved were all dramatically different from those they replaced. Yet, today, many of the transformative technologies that we see being employed are not suddenly doing something we've never seen before. Instead, as Ethan Mollick notes in describing the large language model ChatGPT, "On a technical level, it doesn't work differently than previous AI systems; it's just better at what it does." This year, tech is driven not primarily by new technologies, but by new *integrations* that are more advanced and efficient in using existing technologies. And as this book demonstrates, these trends are further bolstered by the rapid progression of individual component technologies. It makes clear that this year's tech landscape is leading to astonishing changes in how we conduct business and work.

First, natural language models have reached such *advanced* levels—with ChatGPT (released by OpenAI) as the paradigmatic example—that AI-driven capabilities are universally recognized as necessary to transform existing tech products. Within weeks after the release of ChatGPT, for example, Microsoft announced plans to add OpenAI technology to its popular business apps like Word, PowerPoint, and Excel. The company is integrating ChatGPT into its search engine Bing and connecting it with its new image creator, which facilitates creative ways of visualizing new ideas. The speed of integration is happening at a frenzied pace—so fast, in fact, that AI experts and scholars around the globe have expressed grave concerns and sought to pause the development and training of generative AI. Whatever the outcome, one thing seems certain: Generative AI is here to stay and will only continue advancing to become a crucial component in how we approach content creation across diverse industries.

Second, technologies such as AI, AR, and blockchain are being put to work in more *efficient* ways than ever. They help workers perform better, facilitate execution of data-driven tasks, and enhance customers' experiences and engagement. With such improvements, these technologies are now truly starting to uplift the quality of human decision-making and augment performance. This marks a watershed moment: Just as when light bulbs were combined with the electrical grid, or when numerical control tools were integrated into assembly lines, these advances are finally starting to live up to their long-advertised potential. Humans and new technologies can now truly collaborate in ways that can enhance each other's strengths and compensate for each other's weaknesses. For example, ChatGPT can quickly and accurately generate novel combinations of ideas, while humans can use their unique skills to correct, edit, and refine the machine's output in creative ways.

In turn, the business world is positioned to confidently embrace a digital future. Business leaders bold enough to see technological advances as the primary solutions to big problems are met with enthusiasm and legitimate support (see Andy Wu and Goran Calic's chapter on Elon Musk's strategy). They often show little fear in their ambitions to use new technologies in their organizations. Nevertheless, caution is still needed. With the almost endless possibilities for integrative tech applications, we must be cognizant of the challenges that these emerging ways of working bring.

Every digital transformation has two sides. On the one hand, advances in digital technologies promise exciting opportunities to dramatically reinvent your business, unlocking opportunities for increasing productivity, optimizing processes, and creating value. On the other, certain aspects of your business should hold steady—your core identity, your commitment to customers, your attentiveness to employee well-being, and more—so that you do not lose the essence of what makes your business unique. The rapid advancements in technology must not undermine the personal touch and purpose of your company. The key to the success of any digital transformation effort is knowing how to walk this fine line. If you uncritically allow technology to disrupt your company's core identity, you run the risk of coming out on the other side of your digital transformation journey completely distorted in the eyes of your employees, customers, and other stakeholders.

While these AI-enhanced solutions are increasingly being deployed by businesses, it is useful to keep in mind that ever since AI appeared on the business scene, there have been almost continous appeals to focus on our responsibilities in using it. These calls take on renewed urgency in the articles selected for this book. Many of the authors make clear that in a time when we are witnessing a shift toward integrative technologies generating better and higher-quality output and decisions, we need to focus on the new imperatives that have arrived with them. Bringing on technology as a creative collaborator forces us to be aware of the challenges we face with respect to governance, the ethical employment of such technologies, and what it means to be a human in a context of ever-accelerating technological advancement.

With respect to governance, the issue of data management and protection remains a crucial responsibility for organizations. Legal developments are not keeping up with technological advancements, and cybersecurity threats and the sale of stolen data on the dark web are only increasing. In an age where integrative technological progress seems unlimited, we need to put more effort into understanding what it means to use these advances ethically. After all, technologies do not have intentions to do bad or good, nor do they have the moral agency or ability to make judgment calls. These are qualities that are uniquely human, and the responsibilities to exercise them lie with those who are adopting and making use of new integrations.

Altogether, this makes taking care of the potential harms that may emerge from new technological integrations the responsibility of those organizations that deploy them. An example in this book is that, with the arrival of brain sensors, we are now able to measure electrical activity in the brain. Organizations may decide to use this neurotech to track and protect employees from becoming too tired or even burned-out—uses that benefit human well-being. At the same time, however, organizations also need to be aware that the use of wearable brain devices can erode employees' "right to mental privacy" as the sensors provide companies with very intimate and personalized knowledge. Navigating these ethical tightropes requires that those deciding to adopt novel technologies (executives and business leaders) and those responsible for implementing them (IT and HR leaders) need to be trained so that organizations have a digital-ethical savviness to take measures to prevent employee discrimination and ensure safe data management.

A conundrum for business leaders today is that they need to fully embrace new technological developments, but at the same time they must ensure that they use those technologies in ways that serve their employees. This requires maintaining a work culture in which humans are placed first and machines second, but increasingly it seems that leaders are not succeeding. With intelligent machines able to perform complex tasks that were once exclusively handled by highly trained humans, many business leaders see technology as the most important means to solve business problems. They regard investments in technology as a priority over investments in humans, and that is a problem: A "technosolutionism" mindset can prevent organizations from evaluating the use of new technologies from the perspective of what is best for humans.

Of course, to understand fully the potential of these emerging integrative tech solutions, workforces and their leaders must be tech savvy. But an enhanced focus on digital development should not mean less focus on how we develop our employees in their identity and values. To ensure that we use technology in human-centered ways, it will be necessary for companies to invest even more in human upskilling—especially in the face of increasingly shrewd management strategies that favor tech solutions. Upskilling will mean training employees, teams, and their leaders to develop a stronger moral compass to identify the best ways to utilize new technologies without harming the interests of its end users. It also includes training business leaders to incorporate integrative technologies to create work conditions that foster unique human skills such as imagination, critical thinking, creativity, and emotional intelligence.

Perhaps the most important message of this year in tech is that with integrative technologies we have reached a level of technological sophistication that can effectively augment the abilities of employees in ways that will make them *more* instead of *less* human. Our organizations and leaders can achieve such outcomes. The key is to stay informed about what happens around us and reflect on the promising advancements that today's era brings us. The chapters that follow will undoubtedly be helpful to you down this path.

# 1

# NEUROTECH AT WORK

by Nita A. Farahany

The era of brain surveillance has begun. Advances in neuroscience and artificial intelligence are converging to give us an affordable and soon-to-be widely available generation of consumer neurotech devices—a catch-all term for gadgets that, with the help of dry electrodes, connect human brains to computers and the ever-more-sophisticated algorithms that analyze the brain-wave data.

Neuroscientists wrote off earlier iterations of consumer neurotech devices as little better than toys. But as both the hardware and the software have improved, neurotechnology has become more accurate and tougher to dismiss. Today, the global market for neurotech is growing at a compound annual rate of 12% and is expected to reach $21 billion by 2026. This is not a fad. It's a new way of living and thinking about ourselves and our well-being—personally and professionally.

Brain sensors have a rapidly expanding range of personal applications. Using a simple, wearable device that measures electrical activity in the brain or at muscle junctions throughout the body, you can now get graphical, real-time displays of your brain activity and bioelectric changes in your muscles. You can use those displays to "see" your emotions, your arousal, and your alertness. You can learn if you're wired to be conservative or liberal; whether your insomnia is as bad as you think; whether you're in love or just in lust. You can track changes in neurological function over time, such as the slowing down of activity in certain brain regions associated with the onset of conditions such as Alzheimer's disease, schizophrenia, and dementia. If you have epilepsy, you can get advance warning of a seizure so that you can prepare yourself for it. If you're a football player, you'll soon be able to wear a smart helmet that can diagnose concussions immediately after they occur.

Neurotech devices also have a rapidly expanding range of commercial and managerial applications. Companies around the globe have started to integrate neural interfaces into watches, headphones, earbuds, hard hats, caps, and VR headsets for use in the workplace to monitor fatigue, track attention, boost productivity, enhance safety, decrease stress, and create a more responsive working environment. This is new and uncharted territory, full of promise and peril for employers and employees alike. Neurotech devices offer employers ways to improve the well-being and productivity of their employees and thus create healthier, more successful organizations. But they also give employers access to incidental information that can be used to discriminate against employees—for example, information about early cognitive decline. And if employers fail to be transparent about what data they're collecting and why, the devices can undermine employee trust and morale.

Advances in neurotechnology certainly raise significant privacy concerns for employees. Will they know what brain data is being collected or how their employer will use it? Whatever is gained in workplace safety or productivity could be offset by the loss of employee trust, an essential ingredient of corporate success. Employees in high-trust organizations are more productive, have more energy, collaborate better, and are more loyal; employees in low-trust companies feel disempowered and become disengaged. And disengagement matters: It's recently been estimated that corporations in the United States lose $450 billion to $550 billion each year because of it.

The dangers are real. But in some situations—for example, ensuring that the driver of a 40-ton truck is not falling asleep at the wheel—brain monitoring at work seems like a very good idea. It's hard to argue that a driver's right to mental privacy trumps public safety.

To navigate this territory successfully, business leaders need guidance. I've been studying this subject for years. I'm a professor of law and philosophy at Duke University, where I specialize in the legal and ethical issues of emerging technologies, with a particular focus on neurotechnology. I've also served as president of the International Neuroethics Society and cochair of the Neuroethics Working Group for the NIH Brain Initiative, and I currently serve as a neuroethicist for the National Academies of Sciences, Engineering, and Medicine. In this article, I'll provide an overview of the neurotechnology landscape and offer some thoughts on how to balance the risks and benefits of using neurotech devices in the workplace.

It's early days yet, but tens of thousands of workers are already using early-stage devices, and Big Tech is investing heavily to replace peripherals such as the computer mouse and the keyboard with neural interfaces integrated into headsets, earbuds, and wrist-worn devices. So now is the time to start thinking in practical terms about how best to engage with the world that's opening before us, in ways that thoughtfully consider the interests of employees, employers, and society.

# The Lay of the Land

Let's start by taking stock of three ways in which neurotechnology is already being used in the workplace: to track fatigue, to monitor attention and focus, and to adapt the work environment to workers' brains.

## Tracking fatigue

In 2019, Tim Ekert, the CEO of SmartCap, made a bold proclamation. He announced that his company's flagship tool—the LifeBand, a fatigue-tracking headband with embedded EEG sensors that can be worn alone or integrated into a hard hat or cap—would "transform the American trucking industry."

The LifeBand gathers brain-wave data and processes it through SmartCap's LifeApp, which uses proprietary algorithms to assess wearers' fatigue level on a scale from 1 (hyperalert) to 5 (involuntary sleep). When the system detects that a worker is becoming dangerously drowsy, it sends an early warning to both the employee and the manager.

More than 5,000 companies worldwide, in industries such as mining, construction, trucking, and aviation, already use SmartCap to ensure that their employees are wide awake. SmartCap and similar EEG systems can be used in all sorts of employment settings where fatigue negatively affects safety—factory floors, air-traffic-control towers, operating rooms, laboratories, and so on. And safety isn't the only concern: Fatigue also reduces motivation, concentration, and coordination. It slows reaction times, undermines judgment, and impairs workers' ability to carry out even the simplest of mental and physical tasks. It causes some $136 billion in productivity losses a year.

Fatigue also levies catastrophic costs on society. In Chicago, a transit authority train jumped its tracks entering a station at O'Hare International Airport after its driver fell asleep. The train careened onto an escalator, injuring 32 people. In New York, a sleep-deprived train engineer fell asleep while operating a commuter train from Poughkeepsie to Grand Central Terminal in Manhattan. The train took a 30-mph curve at 82 mph and derailed, killing four people, injuring 70, and causing millions of dollars in damage. In Citra, Florida, an engineer fell asleep while operating a train that was pulling 100 railcars full of phosphate and crashed head-on into a coal train. Thirty-two cars left the tracks, spilling 1,346 tons of coal, 1,150 tons of phosphate, 7,400 gallons of diesel fuel, and 77 gallons of battery acid. Aviation accidents are much less common; however, during the past few decades at least 16 major plane crashes have been blamed on pilot fatigue.

As neurotechnology and the algorithms for decoding brain activity continue to improve, neural interfaces will become the gold standard in monitoring fatigue in the workplace. Not just employers but society as a whole may soon decide that the gains in safety and productivity are well worth the costs in employee privacy. But how much we ultimately gain from workplace brain wearables depends largely on how employers use the technology. For example, will employees receive real-time feedback from the devices so that they can act on it themselves, or will managers directly monitor employee fatigue? If so, will they use that information to improve workplace conditions or to justify disciplinary actions, pay cuts, and terminations? The answers to those questions will shape the future of brain-wave monitoring.

Given the lack of societal norms and laws regarding tracking brain activity in general, for now companies are simply creating their own rules about fatigue monitoring. Some use SmartCap and similar technologies to optimize employees' working conditions; others are likely to use the technologies punitively, because that's typically how employers approach workplace surveillance. A recent study of companies that track how their employees use their computers found that 26% of employers had fired workers for misusing the internet and 25% had fired them for misusing email. It's not hard to imagine what might happen when firms are able to regularly monitor not just employees' computers but also their brains.

## Monitoring attention and focus

Many of us lack the ability to focus for long stretches at a time. But Olivier Oullier, a former president of the bioinformatic company Emotiv, believes that neurotechnology can help.

A few years ago, at the *Fortune* Global Tech Forum, Oullier unveiled the MN8, Emotiv's enterprise solution for attention management. The MN8 looks like a set of standard earbuds (and can in fact be used to listen to music or participate in conference calls). But with just two electrodes, one in each ear, the device allows employers to monitor employees' stress and attention levels in real time.

Emotiv teamed up with the German software company SAP to create Focus UX, a system that monitors employees' brain states and in real time shares personalized feedback with them and their managers. SAP predicts that this will create a more responsive workplace environment in which employees focus on what they are best "able to handle at that moment."

To illustrate how the system works, Oullier described a hypothetical situation. A data scientist wearing the MN8 has spent several hours videoconferencing with her team and is now reviewing code. The system has used her alpha-brain-wave activity to index the attentive state in her brain. The proprietary algorithm sees that her attention is flagging, so it sends a message to her laptop: "Christina, it's time for a break. Do you want to take a short walk or do a five-minute guided meditation to reset your focus?"

Focus UX data can be used to evaluate employees' cognitive loads, compare individuals across the workforce, and make decisions about how to optimize the workforce for productivity. It can also help inform decisions about promotion, retention, and firing. Other companies offer similar technology. For example, Lockheed Martin's CogC2 (short for Cognitive Command and Control) provides firms with real-time neurophysiological assessments of employees' workloads so that they can "optimize their workforce for increased productivity and improved employee satisfaction." It's now even possible to use EEG to classify the type of activity an individual is engaged in, according to research funded by the Bavarian State Ministry of Education. As pattern classification of brain-wave data becomes more sophisticated, employers will be able to tell not just whether you are alert or your mind is wandering but also whether you are surfing social media or writing code.

Employers might soon even be able to nudge employees back to work when their minds start to wander. The MIT Media Lab has developed a system called AttentivU, which measures a person's engagement via EEG sensors embedded in a pair of glasses and a wearable scarf. The device provides haptic feedback (usually a form of vibration) whenever the wearer's engagement declines. Researchers found that people who received haptic feedback logged higher alertness scores than those who didn't. While the Media Lab is excited about the results, it acknowledges the risk for misuse, saying it hopes "no one will be forced to use this system, whether in work or school settings."

Some employees may volunteer to use such systems, which have the potential to improve their productivity while giving them control over their brain-activity data. This could allow them to reap the benefits of better time management without any sacrifice of autonomy. As with other neurofeedback approaches, self-monitoring for productivity could also help employees establish better work habits as they learn when and why they get distracted.

The problem is that some organizations may be tempted to impose brain-productivity technology on workers and make attention the currency of productivity measurement. A recent Brookings Institution report found that some companies are now using webcams to track eye movements, body position, and facial expressions as measures of attentiveness to tasks and are reprimanding employees for inattentiveness on the basis of that data. While that kind of monitoring has become increasingly common, especially with the shift to remote work, using attentiveness as a yardstick for employee success may seriously backfire for employers. As Albert Einstein and Isaac Newton both acknowledged, creative ideas depend as much on minds wandering as staying on task. And research across 900 Boston Consulting Group teams in 30 countries has shown that mental downtime increases alertness, improves creativity, and leads to greater output quality. When workers know their attention is being monitored, they may attempt to minimize mental downtime—by doing things to actively bring their attention and focus back to the task at hand—out of a fear of appearing unproductive.

It's not just employees' productivity that can suffer. It's their health too. When employees lack mental downtime, they often experience serious job strain, which has been strongly linked to a variety of health problems: depression and anxiety, ulcers, cardiovascular trouble, and even suicidal thoughts.

Workplace brain surveillance to monitor levels of attention, stress, and other cognitive and emotional functions has stark and significant downsides. It has potential benefits, too, including enhanced employee productivity. But at this point these benefits are purely speculative, so for now I'd recommend that employers steer clear of engaging in this type of brain surveillance.

## Creating more-adaptive work environments

As neurotechnology, AI, and robotics continue to advance, we can expect a future in which brain-activity neural-interface devices are used to make the workplace more adaptive. Penn State researchers, for example, are experimenting with EEG headsets for employees that provide input to robots, which then calibrate their pace of work to the employees' state of mind. In one experiment, participants wore EEG headsets that monitored their cognitive loads and detected signs of stress. Their robotic coworkers reacted to the data by slowing down, speeding up, or keeping a steady pace, giving the workers just the right amount of room to maximize their productivity without stressing them out.

Other researchers have found that EEG sensors could help monitor and address the greater cognitive load that assembly workers bear as automation becomes the norm in industrial settings and they are tasked with increasingly complex assembly procedures. In one recent study, researchers in Belgium had participants perform assembly tasks in a simulated factory setting while being subjected to varying levels of cognitive load (low, high, and overload). The researchers found that by tracking EEG activity and eye movements, they could differentiate between a high cognitive load and cognitive overload, which can produce errors, safety hazards, and detrimental health effects on workers. Smart manufacturing systems of the future could automatically adapt production levels to allow for higher cognitive loads while avoiding overload, ushering in a new era of "cognitive ergonomics."

Some companies are already implementing changes to the workplace in accordance with feedback from employees' brains. Microsoft's Human Factors team, for example, has helped the company adapt its office environments and products to be more responsive to workers' brain health and functioning. Company researchers asked 13 teams of two employees to complete similar tasks together in person and remotely and found that remote collaboration led to greater stress levels in the brain. A second study of employees' brains in back-to-back video meetings versus in-person meetings found that the former were more cognitively stressful.

In response, Microsoft introduced Together mode, a feature in Teams that gives meeting participants a shared background to simulate a shared physical space while collaborating. Initial results are promising: Brain activity of participants in Together mode reflected a lower cognitive burden compared with that of participants using the traditional grid view of online meetings.

The Human Factors team also discovered a simple yet powerful way to address meeting fatigue. By monitoring the brain-wave activity of employees who volunteered to participate, the team learned that people who took short breaks between meetings had lower levels of stress compared with people attending back-to-back meetings. Providing guided brain-wave-based meditation during the breaks also improved well-being and the ability to focus in subsequent meetings.

Cognitive ergonomics—making the workplace safer, more responsive, and more adaptive to employees' well-being—represents one of the most promising new applications of neurotechnology. In my view, companies should embrace opportunities to experiment with it.

## Using Brain Wearables Responsibly

To reap the maximum benefits from brain wearables in the workplace while minimizing the risks, firms must adopt policies and practices that specify how and when they are used. To start, this will require action in five key areas.

## 1. Employee rights

Employees have a right to mental privacy. Governments should codify that as part of the international human right to privacy. A right to mental privacy would place the burden on corporations to identify a specific use for brain wearables that is limited in scope to legitimate purposes, such as monitoring fatigue in commercial drivers or tracking attention in air traffic controllers. A right to mental privacy would also prohibit unauthorized access to other brain-wave data that may be collected incidentally during legal monitoring. Even then, companies should be prohibited from using data for any purpose other than the one it was originally gathered for.

## 2. Privacy laws and regulation

Employers should stay abreast of biometrics privacy laws and implement policies consistent with their requirements. The collection of brain-wave data is or soon will be subject to stringent privacy laws and regulatory requirements in some U.S. jurisdictions. The failure to obtain prior written consent and provide adequate disclosure to employees can have costly financial and reputational implications for employers. In October 2022, for example, employees in a class-action lawsuit that included nearly 45,000 people were awarded $228 million in a jury verdict against BNSF Railway, one of the largest freight railroad networks in North America, because it had collected and stored fingerprint data in violation of the Illinois Biometric Information Privacy Act. Given the unique liability risks associated with the collection of biometric brain data, companies planning to introduce neurotechnology in the workplace should carefully consider laws enacted in various U.S. states and in other countries, including the General Data Protection Regulation in Europe.

## 3. Terms of use

When appropriate, employers should offer employees the opportunity to use brain wearables at work to monitor their own levels of stress, waning attention, or increasing cognitive load. Companies may also choose to offer guided meditation and other neurofeedback tools to employees who would like to improve their well-being. If employees elect to use those tools, firms should not access or mine the neural data collected, unless employees explicitly consent to its use for a specified purpose. Employees must have a right to obtain a copy of any neural data collected about them, along with any interpretations drawn from it. To use these tools without consent constitutes a breach of trust, undermining the value they would otherwise create. Giving employees the right to audit their own brain data can help build trust and ensure that only relevant and legitimate brain data is collected. It also provides a check on the quality of the data being collected and an opportunity for employees to challenge invalid interpretations.

## 4. Disclosure

Regardless of biometric-data-collection laws or other regulations, employers should be transparent with employees about what data they're collecting from brain wearable devices and how they intend to use that information. They should specify the purpose for which brain data is being collected and what actions they will take in response to insights drawn from it. They should also collect data from brain wearables only when the employee is working. If, for example, an employer issues headphones embedded with EEG sensors, and the employee is permitted to use those headphones not just for work but also for leisure activities, employers should not collect neural data during "off" hours.

# 5. Storing brain data

Employers should adopt best practices for data minimization and store brain data on employees' own devices and not on servers of device manufacturers, software companies, or employers whenever possible. This is critical. People associate their sense of self most closely with the information in their own minds, which makes neural data particularly sensitive. As machine-learning algorithms improve, the ability to mine and interpret neural data will also improve, enabling firms to learn far more about what employees are feeling or thinking and about cognitive or affective changes to their brains over time. Employers should adopt security safeguards against the risk of unauthorized access, destruction, disclosure, or use of neural data. For example, companies should make sure that brain data is "overwritten" once its limited purpose has been served.

. . .

Neural interfaces will increasingly compete with existing peripheral devices to become one of the primary ways people interact with technology, offering firms powerful new insights into employees and their well-being, and revealing ways to make workplaces safer and more productive. To realize those benefits, employers must understand the unique risks this technology poses to mental privacy and adopt clear workplace policies that empower employees and earn the trust of the future workforce.

**TAKEAWAYS**

The global market for neurotech is growing rapidly, enabling new ways of living and thinking—personally and professionally. Companies should now begin to explore the risks and benefits of using neurotech devices in the workplace.

✓ Neurotechnology is already being used at work in three main ways: to track fatigue, to monitor attention and focus, and to adapt work the environment to employees' brains.

✓ To realize the benefits of neurotech, employers must understand the unique risks this technology poses to mental privacy and adopt clear workplace policies.

✓ Earning employees' trust will require action in five key areas: employee rights, privacy laws and regulation, terms of use, disclosure, and brain data storage.

*Adapted from an article in* Harvard Business Review, *March–April 2023 (product #S23022). Nita A. Farahany is the author of* The Battle for Your Brain: Defending the Right to Think Freely in the Age of Neurotechnology *(St. Martin's Press 2023), from which this article is adapted.*

# 2

# WHY BUILD IN WEB3

by Jad Esber and Scott Duke Kominers

Today's dominant internet platforms are built on aggregating users and user data. As these platforms have grown, so has their ability to provide value—thanks to the power of network effects—which has enabled them to stay ahead. For example, Facebook's (now Meta's) data on user behavior helped it fine-tune its algorithms to a point that its content feed and ad targeting were dramatically better than what competitors could offer. Amazon, meanwhile, has exploited its broad view into customer demand to both optimize delivery logistics and develop its own product lines. And YouTube has built a massive library of videos from a wide array of creators, enabling it to offer viewers content on almost any topic.

In these business models, locking in users and their data is a key source of competitive advantage. As a result, traditional internet platforms typically do not share data even in aggregate—and they make it difficult for users to export their social graphs and other content. So, even if users grow dissatisfied with a given platform, it's often not worth it to leave.

But all of this might be changing. While it's hard for newcomers to challenge "Web 2.0" companies like Meta on their own terms, now companies—working in what they're calling a "Web3" model—are proposing a novel value proposition. Despite all the public conversations around the metaverse and various hyper-financialized NFT projects, Web3, more than anything, is a fundamentally different approach that some developers have agreed to. It's based on the premise that there's an alternative to exploiting users for data to make money—and that instead, building open platforms that share value with users directly will create more value for everyone, including the platform.

In Web3, instead of platforms having full control of the underlying data, users typically own whatever content they have created (such as posts or videos), as well as digital objects they have purchased. Moreover, these digital assets are typically created according to interoperable standards on public blockchains, instead of being privately hosted on a company's servers. This makes the assets "portable," in the sense that a user can, in principle, leave any given platform whenever they want by unplugging from that app and moving—along with their data—to another one.

This is a major shift, which could fundamentally change how digital companies operate: Users' ability to take their data from one platform to another introduces new sources of competitive pressure, and likely requires firms to update their business strategies. If a platform isn't creating enough value for its users, they might simply leave. And indeed, in Web3, new entrants can explicitly incentivize power users to move to them—for instance, the NFT trading platform LooksRare recently launched through what's called a "vampire attack," a Web3 phenomenon in which one platform "sucks" participants away from another platform, rewarding people for switching over from the dominant platform OpenSea.

But at the same time, the dynamics of Web3 are less zero-sum, which means a platform's overall value creation opportunity can be bigger. Building on an interoperable infrastructure layer makes it easy for platforms to plug into broader content networks, thereby expanding the scale and types of value they can provide their users. A Web3 art gallery, for example, can bootstrap off the artwork users have already created on the blockchain, rather than requiring them to upload art to the platform directly.

This can be a valuable approach to sourcing content even for established platforms. Twitter recently introduced a feature whereby users can show NFTs they own in their profiles; Instagram is working on something similar. And for new platforms, the ability to integrate preexisting digital assets can be critical in resolving what's called the "cold-start problem"—the reality that it can be challenging for a platform to get momentum early on because of a lack of initial content.

Moreover, the infrastructure layer means that the costs associated with creating user trust are much lower in Web3. Managing digital assets on public ledgers makes it clearer which assets exist and who owns what, which was previously a struggle on the web. If a digital artist, for example, claims that a new artwork is limited to 489 editions, then prospective owners can verify that on the blockchain directly—without needing to trust the artist themself, or having a gallery or other intermediary provide such an assurance.

This trust framework extends to the software that runs Web3 platforms: Key operations can be encoded on the blockchain in "smart contracts" that are auditable and immutable. This makes it possible for a platform designer to commit up front to certain design features, such as pricing rules, royalty agreements, and user reward mechanics.

All of this means that—at least in theory—it can be much easier to launch a product in Web3. Even an unknown entrepreneur can build products that plug into an existing network without permission from an established platform. Indeed, taken to the limit, in Web3, users sometimes have no need to trust the company (or people) behind a project; rather, they just have to trust the code itself. Some fundraising campaigns supporting humanitarian aid efforts in Ukraine, for example, were run through smart contracts that automatically transfer all funds received to the Ukrainian government or associated charities; this means donors can trust that their funds will be used properly even if the campaign organizers are completely anonymous.

Of course, given the early financial use cases of Web3 and the high volume of transactions, a number of bad actors have leveraged the hype to orchestrate scams. Many of the Web3 experiences today were designed for tech-savvy power users, whereas ordinary users might have only a limited understanding of what an app or platform can actually do, much less be able to vet source code to verify that it functions as described. There's a long way to go before Web3 technology is safe and accessible to the average consumer.

Furthermore, plugging into an existing network in practice doesn't mean you can automatically unlock an engaged user base that wants to stick around. Just as in all entrepreneurial ventures, it's essential to build a product that solves for a true user need. But once you *have* solved a user need, leveraging established networks through Web3 makes it much easier to deploy and scale.

Making platform backends open and interoperable enables compounding innovation and incentivizes direct investment in building the infrastructure layers. For example, koodos—a Web3 service that lets people create collections of things they love from across the internet—is building shared infrastructure that any network can plug into and improve. (Disclosure: Esber cofounded koodos, and Kominers provides market design advice to the company.)

Sharing infrastructure means that apps can focus on building great experiences, driving toward a greater emphasis on platform design as a source of competitive advantage. What an app has understood about its market manifests in its user experience and interface—and so even in Web3, the insights consumer apps generate about their users will continue to differentiate them.

Web3 platforms also have the potential to unlock a novel and especially powerful form of network effect through community engagement and social cohesion.

Ownership of digital assets fosters a sense of psychological ownership that can make consumers feel so invested in a product that it becomes almost an extension of themselves. A platform's users literally become "fans" who form a bond through the shared platform experience—similar to how fans of a sports team or obscure band see themselves as a community.

For example, The Hundreds, a popular streetwear brand, sold NFTs themed around its mascot, the "Adam Bomb." Holding one of these NFTs gives access to community events and exclusive merchandise, providing a way for the brand's fans to meet and engage with each other—and thus reinforcing their enthusiasm. The Hundreds also spontaneously announced that it would pay royalties (in store credit) to owners of the NFTs associated with Adam Bomb that were used in some of its clothing collections. This made it roughly as if you could have part ownership in the Ralph Lauren emblem, and every new line of polos that used that emblem would give you a dividend. Partially decentralizing the brand's value in this way led everyone in The Hundreds's community to feel even more attached to the IP and to go out of their way to promote it—to the point that some community members even got Adam Bomb tattoos.

Another example is SushiSwap, which is a "fork" of the decentralized finance platform Uniswap—meaning

SushiSwap's underlying algorithms are a clone of the code that Uniswap published. The main difference is that SushiSwap set up a strong brand and community, alongside an active and ongoing reward system for users that drove higher user engagement and positive sentiment about the platform; this then enabled it to quickly emerge as a successful competitor to Uniswap.

More generally, sharing ownership allows for more incentive alignment between products and their derivatives, creating incentives for everyone to become a builder and contributor. The underlying technology standards also enable every Web3 company to be built upon. This means the community around a platform can cocreate in a way that's much less adversarial than in the past and with more derivatives in circulation—making the platform ecosystem grow even stronger.

In the short run, this model gives up some share of consumer surplus to the builder or creator. But because the builders get more, they're strongly incentivized to invest and grow the total pie for everyone, which means that in the long run, Web3 should raise consumer surplus as well.

. . .

Web3 has the potential to unlock a more valuable internet for everyone. New companies can build on Web3 infrastructure to create communities around their brands and product concepts much more easily than in previous iterations of the web. And even established platforms can leverage these forces by plugging into blockchain-based content networks and giving their users some ownership over their data. All of this means that the next era of the web will likely look a lot different—and more open— than the one we're living with today.

TAKEAWAYS

Today's dominant internet platforms have guarded their troves of user data and maintained an advantage through network effects. Companies using Web3 have a new value proposition for users.

✓ In Web3, users—not platforms—own whatever content they have created, as well as digital objects they have purchased, and these digital assets are typically portable.

✓ This new paradigm makes it easier for new companies to compete with established ones if they offer better user experience.

✓ Because the system is less zero-sum than Web2.0, user lock-in isn't the primary goal for platforms. A platform's overall value creation opportunity can be bigger.

✓ The costs associated with creating user trust are much lower in Web3. Managing digital assets on public ledgers makes it clearer which assets exist and who owns what.

✓ These features taken together may mean that it will be easier to launch a product in Web3—users just have to trust a project's code, not necessarily the company or people behind it.

*Adapted from content posted on hbr.org, May 16, 2022 (product #H0713Z).*

## 3

# CHATGPT IS A TIPPING POINT FOR AI

by Ethan Mollick

n December 2022, OpenAI released ChatGPT, a powerful new chatbot that can communicate in plain English using an updated version of its AI system. While versions of GPT have been around for a while, this model has crossed a threshold: It's genuinely useful for a wide range of tasks, from creating software to generating business ideas to writing a wedding toast. While previous generations of the system could technically do these things, the quality of the outputs was much lower than that produced by an average human. The new model is much better, often startlingly so.

Put simply: This is a *very* big deal. The businesses that understand the significance of this change—and act on it first—will be at a considerable advantage. Especially as ChatGPT is just the first of many similar chatbots that will soon be available, and they are increasing in capacity exponentially every year.

At first glance, ChatGPT might seem like a clever toy. On a technical level, it doesn't work differently than previous AI systems, it's just better at what it does. Since its release, Twitter has been flooded with examples of people using it to strange and absurd ends: writing weight-loss plans and children's books and offering advice on how to remove a peanut butter sandwich from a VCR in the style of the King James Bible.

There are other reasons to be skeptical besides the unusual use cases. Most pointedly, despite years of hype, AI notoriously only sort of works in most applications outside of data analysis. It's pretty good at steering cars, but sometimes it rams into another vehicle. Mostly, it provides good answers to queries, but sometimes it seems to make up the results entirely.

But a deeper exploration reveals much more potential. And the more you look, the more you see what has changed with this model—and why it seems like a tipping point.

ChatGPT, now open to everyone, has made an important transition. Until now, AI has primarily been aimed at problems where failure is expensive, not at tasks where occasional failure is cheap and acceptable—or even ones in which experts can easily separate failed cases from successful ones. A car that occasionally gets into accidents is intolerable. But an AI artist that draws some great pictures, but also some bad ones, is perfectly acceptable. Applying AI to the creative and expressive tasks (writing marketing copy) rather than dangerous and repetitive ones (driving a forklift) opens a new world of applications.

What are those applications, and why do they matter so much?

First, not only can this AI produce paragraphs of solidly written English (or French, or Mandarin, or whatever language you choose) with a high degree of sophistication, it can also create blocks of computer code on command. To give you an idea of what this looks like, I introduced my undergraduate entrepreneurship students to the new AI system and before I was done talking, one of my students had used it to create the code for a startup prototype using code libraries they had never seen before. They completed a four-hour project in less than an hour.

This is a major change. Massive increases in speed have been seen in a randomized trial of AI code tools.[1] One good programmer can now legitimately do what not so long ago was the work of many, and people who have never programmed will soon be able to create workable code as well.

Second, it has an incredible capacity to perform different kinds of writing with more significant implications than might be initially apparent. The use of AI in writing can greatly increase the productivity of businesses in a variety of industries. By utilizing AI's ability to quickly and accurately generate written content, businesses can save time and resources, allowing them to focus on other important tasks. This is particularly beneficial for industries such as marketing and advertising, consulting, and finance, where high-quality written materials are essential for communicating with clients and stakeholders. Additionally, AI can also be useful for industries such as journalism and publishing, where it can help generate articles and other written content with speed and accuracy. Overall, the use of AI in writing will greatly benefit businesses by allowing them to produce more written materials in less time.

An AI wrote the previous paragraph. It also actively revised it in response to my criticism to improve the material. (See figure 3-1 for details.) In tests of whether it

FIGURE 3-1

# More written materials in less time

**Prompt: Give some examples of the types of writing AI can do, and why that will transform businesses, in a paragraph.**

Response: AI can be used to write a wide range of business-related documents, including reports, proposals, and marketing materials. By utilizing AI's ability to generate ideas and provide information, businesses can quickly and easily create high-quality written materials. This can save time and resources, allowing businesses to focus on other important tasks. Additionally, AI can help ensure accuracy and consistency in writing, improving the overall professionalism and effectiveness of business documents. The use of AI in writing will transform businesses by streamlining the writing process and improving the quality and accuracy of written materials.

**Give clear examples of the types of businesses that will be impacted in the paragraph.**

AI can have a significant impact on a variety of businesses, including marketing and advertising agencies, consulting firms, and financial institutions. These businesses often rely on high-quality written materials, such as reports, proposals, and marketing campaigns, to communicate with clients and stakeholders. By utilizing AI's ability to quickly and accurately generate written content, these businesses can save time and resources while improving the effectiveness of their written materials. Additionally, AI can help ensure consistency and accuracy in writing, further enhancing the professionalism and credibility of the business. Overall, the use of AI in writing will greatly benefit businesses in these industries by streamlining the writing process and improving the quality of written materials.

**Instead of focusing on credibility, focus on how much more work can get done and give an additional type of industry impacted by AI writing. Make the paragraph more interesting.**

The use of AI in writing can greatly increase the productivity of businesses in a variety of industries. By utilizing AI's ability to quickly and accurately generate written content, businesses can save time and resources, allowing them to focus on other important tasks. This is particularly beneficial for industries such as marketing and advertising, consulting, and finance, where high-quality written materials are essential for communicating with clients and stakeholders. Additionally, AI can also be useful for industries such as journalism and publishing, where it can help generate articles and other written content with speed and accuracy. Overall, the use of AI in writing will greatly benefit businesses by allowing them to produce more written materials in less time.

could make other parts of my job as a professor easier, it took seconds to write a reasonable course syllabus, class assignments, grading criteria, even lecture notes that could be potentially useful with some editing.[2]

This highlights the third major change that happened with this release: the possibility of human-machine hybrid work. Instead of prompting an AI and hoping for a good result, humans can now guide AIs and correct mistakes. (Despite what my AI writing partner claims above, it's not *always* accurate.) This means experts will be able to fill in the gaps of the AI's capability, even as the AI becomes more helpful to the expert. This sort of interaction has led to increases in the performance of players of Go, one of the world's oldest and most complex games, who have learned from the AIs that mastered the sport and become unprecedentedly better players themselves.

A final reason why this will be transformative: The limits of the current language model are completely unknown. Using the public mode, people have used ChatGPT to do basic consulting reports, write lectures, produce code that generates novel art, generate ideas, and much more. Using specialized data, it's possible to build each customer their own customized AI that predicts what they need, responds to them personally, and remembers all their interactions.

This isn't science fiction. It is entirely doable with the technology just released.

The problems of AI remain very real, however. For one, it is a consummate bullshitter, and I mean that in a technical sense. Bullshit is convincing-sounding nonsense, devoid of truth, and AI is very good at creating it. You can ask it to describe how we know dinosaurs had a civilization and it will happily make up a whole set of facts explaining, quite convincingly, exactly that. It is no replacement for Google. It literally does not know what it doesn't know, because it is, in fact, not an entity at all, but rather a complex algorithm generating meaningful sentences.

It also can't explain what it does or how it does it, making the results of AI inexplicable. That means that systems can have biases and that unethical action is possible, hard to detect, and hard to stop. When ChatGPT was released, you couldn't ask it to tell you how to rob a bank, but you could ask it to write a one-act play about how to rob a bank, or to explain it for "educational purposes," or to write a program explaining how to rob a bank, and it would happily do those things. These issues will become more acute as these tools spread.

But these disadvantages are much more prevalent outside of the creative, analytical, and writing-based work that AI is now capable of. A writer can easily edit badly written sentences that may appear in AI articles, a human programmer can spot errors in AI code, and an analyst can check the results of AI conclusions. This leads us, ultimately, to why this is so disruptive. The writer no longer needs to write the articles alone, the programmer to code on their own, or the analyst to approach the data themselves. The work is a new kind of collaboration that did not exist last month. One person can do the work of many, and that is even without the additional capabilities that AI provides.

This is why the world has suddenly changed. The traditional boundaries of jobs have suddenly shifted. Machines can now do tasks that could only be done by highly trained humans. Some valuable skills are no longer useful, and new skills will take their place. And no one really knows what any of this means yet. And keep in mind: This is just one of *many* models like this that are in the works, from both companies you know, like Google, and others you may not.

So, after reading this article, I hope you immediately start experimenting with AI and start high-level discussions about the implications: for your company, your industry, and the rest of the world. Integrating AI into our work—and our lives—will bring sweeping changes. Right now, we're just scratching the surface of what those might be.

**TAKEAWAYS**

With ChatGPT and other tools that can communicate in plain English, draft and revise text, and write code, generative AI technology is suddenly becoming more useful to a broader segment of the population. This has huge implications, and we're just scratching the surface of what those might be.

✓ The ability to generate text and code on command means people are capable of producing more work, faster than ever before. ChatGPT's ability to produce different kinds of writing means it's useful for many different kinds of businesses.

✓ Its capacity to respond to feedback and revise its own work means there's significant potential for hybrid human/AI work.

✓ We don't yet know the limits of these new AI models. All of this could mean sweeping changes for how—and what—work is done in the near future.

## NOTES

1.  Eirini Kalliamvakou, "Research: Quantifying GitHub Copilot's Impact on Developer Productivity and Happiness," GitHub blog, September 7, 2022, https://github.blog/2022-09-07-research -quantifying-github-copilots-impact-on-developer-productivity -and-happiness/.

2.  Ethan Mollick, "The Mechanical Professor," *One Useful Thing* (blog), December 6, 2022, https://oneusefulthing.substack.com/p /the-mechanical-professor.

*Adapted from content posted on hbr.org, December 14, 2022 (product #H07EWB).*

4

# LEVERAGING NEW TECH TO BRING SUPPLY CHAINS CLOSER TO HOME

by Suketu Gandhi

The location of low-cost labor largely shaped today's global supply chains, but that has changed dramatically over the past five years. Technology is finally ready to replace human labor across a broad range of supply chain activities, which will give companies more opportunities to operate where they choose and reduce their dependence on Asia.

Savvy companies are busily exploring how they can employ a host of new technologies to make their end-to-end supply chain much more resilient yet still competitively cost-efficient. Those that succeed will take an artificial intelligence plus human intelligence (AI + HI) approach. But first, they will revisit what customers really value and bring the supply chains for higher-margin products closer to home.

## The Current Challenge

Today's global supply chains were designed to operate reliably at the lowest possible cost in a steady-state environment. Lately, however, they have been unreliable, such as with the microchip shortage, and expensive, including with higher costs for labor, commodities, and ocean shipping—primarily because conditions have been anything but steady.[1] Geopolitical tensions between the Western democracies and the autocracies of Russia and China have led to calls for companies to become less vulnerable by radically restructuring their distant supply chains.

Companies have long expressed interest in reshoring, near-shoring (switching to suppliers closer to the markets served), and friend-shoring (using suppliers located in countries with shared values)—all of which offer certain logistical, strategic, and brand image advantages. The biggest obstacles have been labor costs, labor availability, and deep manufacturing expertise. The largest and most affordable pool of qualified manufacturing labor is in China and other low-cost Asian countries. But advances in technology are starting to lower these barriers.

## New Technologies

A few developments are beginning to make a difference. For example, it is possible to locate affordable factories closer to home. Companies are also improving their operations and reducing the time it takes to train workers from months to days on tasks such as assembling diverse products—electrical or mechanical—on the same assembly line.

AI + HI. The maturity of AI, particularly humans' ability to use it, offers new ways out of the cost trap. Major advances in *cobots*—robots that directly interact with humans in manufacturing facilities—combine AI and HI to lower labor costs while retaining the value of human oversight.

3D printing. Advances in additive manufacturing (3D printing) are making it possible for companies to affordably produce a broad range of components and products. They are also allowing them to shorten manufacturing processes in factories closer to home, reducing reliance on numerous and distant suppliers.

Recognition technology. In manual manufacturing processes, such as automobile engine assembly, AI-driven action recognition technology combines live video with analytics to ensure that workers are correctly following complicated steps without making errors. The result is better quality control, higher productivity, and datasets that can be used to improve processes.

Digital manufacturing solutions. These systems track product manufacturing across workstations, enable real-time input of data by workers, provide end-to-end traceability, and ensure that only high-quality parts move downstream.

3D simulation. This includes metaverse applications such as Nvidia's Omniverse. Simulations allow manufacturers to build digital twins of their processes and simulate factory layouts, workstation designs, and assembly design.

Logistics technology. Investments are pouring into this area, especially in tools for warehouse management, matching freight loads to transportation capacity, and cost-effective routing. The rate of investment from venture capital (VC) firms suggests that VC funding for "supply tech" will overtake that for fintech before the end of this decade.

Three moves can help companies take full advantage of these labor-saving intelligent technologies:

## Rethink what customers really value

Start with deep analysis of what customers will want, where they will want it, and when. Many products are complex in places where consumers do not see value but production is labor-intensive—issues that mattered less when supply chains were stable and labor costs low. Recognizing this, some companies are moving toward making products in smaller batches that are keyed to refined customer preferences. Some are finding ways to adapt or redesign products for automated production without sacrificing perceived or effective end-user value.

Consider a manufacturer of industrial tools that had seen its products grow more complex with many subcomponents, such as motors, switches, controllers, and wiring, and many raw materials, such as resins, plastics, and copper. Before bringing manufacturing from Asia and closer to most of their customers in North America and Europe, the company took a hard look at what its customers really cared about. It found that, above all, users wanted a motor that lasted a long time and a tool that could survive in a harsh operating environment. The company was able to eliminate many of its products' superfluous elements, making manufacturing easier to automate and less expensive while still delivering the attributes that customers wanted.

## Rebalance machine intelligence with human agency

AI, analytics, and robotics can greatly reduce reliance on human effort to move products through value chains faster, more reliably, and more efficiently. But the goal should not be to remove human beings completely from processes; it should be to free them to do what they do best: make critical judgments based on their experience and expertise. For example, these technologies can allow workers to devote more time to investigating and learning from system failures and figuring out how to make the system more robust.

Consider a medical device manufacturer. In its industry, safety is the number one priority, and getting the product to the customer rapidly is number two. There is tension between these priorities. Reshoring would help get products to customers faster but increase labor costs. So the company adopted machine learning and state-of-the-art cameras to inspect for anomalies in the products and in the manufacturing process. The company's best human experts then identify the causes.

## Bring newer, higher-margin products closer to home first

When companies first began moving manufacturing to low-cost countries, they usually focused first on their high-volume, lower-margin products. Now, as they relocate production closer to home and to customers, they should begin with their higher-margin products for three reasons.

First, because higher-margin products are often more complex (such as medical devices), using new technologies to produce them and to manage their supply chains can generate the most benefits.

Second, in the face of today's uncertain global supply chains, companies should take into account the risks of disruptions for all of their products and make the repatriation of those that deliver the highest return the priority.

Third, thin margins leave no financial room for experimentation, learning, and the initial capital expenditure needed to maneuver in a world of new technology and higher labor costs. As a result, it's difficult to make the business case for a move, and companies are paralyzed. But when relocation is considered in terms of the total amount of margin repatriated instead of total cost savings, the business case becomes compelling. And as a company continually improves its manufacturing proficiency with higher-margin products, it can then turn its attention to relocating the manufacture of lower-margin products.

Admittedly, making all these changes will take time. Companies will not be able to drastically reduce their dependence on suppliers in China and other distant countries overnight. But by understanding the capabilities of these technologies and aggressively investing in them, companies will be able to bolster the resilience of their supply chains in the months and years ahead.

TAKEAWAYS

Today's global supply chains were designed to operate with high reliability, at the lowest possible cost, in a steady-state environment. During the pandemic supply chains became more erratic and expensive, but the emergence of new technologies is making supply chains more resilient.

✓ New developments in technology—including AI + human intelligence, 3D printing, recognition technology, digital manufacturing solutions, and 3D simulations—are making it possible for Western countries to relocate factories closer to home, lowering supply chain risk.

✓ To remove complexity from supply chains, companies should rethink what customers really value and simplify products' superfluous elements.

✓ Companies should bring higher-margin products closer to home first. These products are typically more complex and more exposed to supply chain risk.

## NOTES

1. Jason Furman and Wilson Powell III, "Record US Productivity Slump in First Half of 2022 Risks Higher Inflation and Unemployment," *PIEE* (blog), August 9, 2022, https://www.piie.com/blogs/realtime-economics/record-us-productivity-slump-first-half-2022-risks-higher-inflation-and; CMO Pink Sheet, September 2022, World Bank, https://thedocs.worldbank.org/en/doc/5d903e848db1d1b83e0ec8f744e55570-0350012021/related/CMO-Pink-Sheet-September-2022.pdf; Yan Carrière-Swallow et al.,

"How Soaring Shipping Costs Raise Prices Around the World," *IMF* (blog), March 28, 2022, https://www.imf.org/en/Blogs /Articles/2022/03/28/how-soaring-shipping-costs-raise-prices -around-the-world.

*Adapted from content posted on hbr.org, October 26, 2022 (product #H079ZF).*

# 5

# YOUR COMPANY'S DATA IS FOR SALE ON THE DARK WEB. SHOULD YOU BUY IT BACK?

by Brenda R. Sharton

One day I got a call from the in-house counsel at a large financial institution. "Our [information security] team was doing a routine search and found a list of our employee passwords for sale on the dark web," she told me. "The business folks want to buy it back. What should we do? Should we buy it ourselves? Are there any downsides?"

I get calls like this frequently, and the short answer is that, in most cases, the legal and reputational risks far outweigh the benefits of purchasing the information. Cybercriminals frequently use the dark web—a hub of criminal and illicit activity—to sell data from companies that they have gained unauthorized access to through credential stuffing attacks, phishing attacks, hacking, or even leaks from a company insider.

The legal and reputational risks include:

## It drives up the price of your company data and puts a target on your back

If you purchase your company's data, it could not only make the data itself more expensive—you also risk getting a reputation as a company that will pay up, making you an even more desirable target for future cyber extortion and ransom attacks.

Even if cybercriminals are unaware that your company is the purchaser, they will still note that the data is selling. If they do know your company is the buyer, they may publicize this in their own circles, putting your company at further reputational risk.

## You don't know what you're getting with or in that data

It's inherently risky to purchase data from the dark web, as you're invariably buying it from untrustworthy characters—either threat actors or someone who has purchased it illicitly from the hackers. The data may have malicious code within it or contain a Trojan horse that potentially could provide cybercriminals with unauthorized access to company systems.

## The data may contain confidential or proprietary information from other companies

Sellers may be offering your company's data in combination with data from other sources, including your competitors or business partners. You won't know this until it's too late. The owners of that data could then claim your company has breached confidentiality agreements or other laws (misappropriation of trade secrets or worse, receipt of stolen property).

## Your purchase could trigger notification obligations and increase regulatory risk

Purchasing the data could provide you with evidence that your data had been exfiltrated, which would trigger reporting requirements to consumers and regulators, opening you up to the risk of litigation and enforcement actions. At best, you're put in the difficult position of determining whether regulatory notices are triggered or taking the chance that a regulator later will claim that it should have been notified.

## Your purchase might even violate U.S. sanctions

Because it's difficult to be sure of the seller's identity, purchasing the data may open your company up to liability for violating Treasury Department rules if the threat actors are associated with sanctioned countries. The U.S. Department of the Treasury's Office of Foreign Assets Control (OFAC) brings enforcement actions against businesses that make payments to threat actors when those payments constitute U.S. sanctions violations.

## Even if you use a third-party purchaser, your company still may have exposure

A third-party service will then have access to your company's customer, vendor, and employee data, putting that data at additional risk. And you may still be open to liability for directing the payment.

## You may be sued by individuals whose data was exposed

You may be legally obligated to provide notice to individuals that you've found their data on the dark web. These individuals may accuse your company of not properly safeguarding their data, perhaps unfairly assuming the breach was of company systems or as a result of company fault. This could lead to a loss of business and possible lawsuits.

## The information may still live on the dark web

Given that you're dealing with cybercriminals or their associates, there's no guarantee that the purchase will lead to the data being completely safeguarded. The seller may not have possession or control of all copies of your stolen data and would therefore be unable to prevent further sale or dissemination. Or they might continue to sell your data to others themselves.

Purchasing data unrelated to your company's business from the dark web is inadvisable for many of the same reasons discussed above. Your company would be exposing itself to the risk of receiving stolen information or even trade secrets of competitors, creating both legal and reputational risk. There is no scenario under which this would be advisable.

We recognize that there may be certain circumstances in which your company would still consider purchasing information off the dark web. These purchases should be very rare and made with extreme caution. In these circumstances, an OFAC analysis should be done as well to decrease the risk that you are purchasing data from a sanctioned country or individual.

TAKEAWAYS

In the course of monitoring, you may come across your company's proprietary information on the dark web.

Should you try to buy it back? In most cases, the legal and reputational risks far outweigh the benefits of paying for your stolen data.

✓ It drives up the price of your company data and puts a target on your back. Additionally, you may be sued by individuals whose data was exposed.

✓ You don't know what you're getting with or in that data. It may even contain confidential or proprietary information from other companies.

✓ Your purchase could trigger notification obligations and increase regulatory risk or even violate international sanctions.

✓ Even if you use a third-party purchaser, your company still may have exposure and the information may still live on the dark web.

*Adapted from content posted on hbr.org, January 4, 2023 (product #H07F4F).*

# 6

# HOW ONE AIRLINE IS USING AR TO IMPROVE OPERATIONS

by Ting Li, Jason Wang, and Fei Wu

Technologies sometimes take a surprisingly long time to catch on, despite their obvious potential. Augmented reality (AR) is a case in point. Although we have had the means to support visual information overlays for nearly a decade (think Google Glass), it's only now that businesses are beginning to figure out how to take full advantage of its capabilities.

Consider how the landscape is changing. Right now, thousands of experiments in what might be called augmented operations are underway at companies all over the world. One of the biggest is taking place at China Southern Airlines (CSA), where the team at the company's technical arm, China Southern Technic, have woven augmented reality, artificial intelligence, cloud computing, the internet of things, and 5G connectivity into a single application that can extend human capacities, enhance safety, and improve performance.

## Safety 2.0

One of the first processes to benefit from CSA's embrace of the augmented reality is the safety inspection. (While the cause of the 2022 crash of a Boeing 737 operated by China Eastern Airlines is still being investigated, the incident underscores the importance of using any and all safety inspection tools available.)

After every landing of any passenger aircraft anywhere in the world, a maintenance, repair, and operations (MRO) engineer must perform a thorough aircraft inspection. An inspection on a Boeing 737 typically takes more than 100 steps, and an Airbus 320 takes more than 200 steps. This is a basic but crucial part of airline management, a pressing task that frontline MRO engineers must perform every day, often a number of times. CSA is no exception. As the world's third-largest airline, CSA repeats this procedure over 2,500 times a day, a task that takes the airline's MRO engineers about 1,000 worker hours.

In most of the world's airports, engineers check off each inspection item on a bulky, paper-based job card, a block of 20-plus sheets of paper that they have to clutch throughout the entire task. Until recently, CSA's MRO engineers worked this way too, performing this work while juggling paper, pens, walkie-talkies, and the job card. But now, at 22 airports CSA flies out of, most of the information, recordkeeping, and communications tools are integrated into a single AR display. This display puts a whole range of resources at the engineers' service—not only text, but images, videos, graphs, and voice, in any combination that is helpful to the engineers.

While the AR glasses are expected to shave 6% off those 1,000 daily hours, we have found in our research on the integration of this technology at CSA that the advantages of the AR glasses go far beyond the labor dividend. They aren't just a new way to get information—they're a whole new way of working.

CSA's AR glasses allow engineers to edit and reorganize their job list and change the information they see and how they want it shown. Their displays can be adjusted by aircraft, season, and even individual preference. They offer the engineers step-by-step multimedia support and immersive experiences during the execution of the tasks, including AI object recognition and collaboration with a remote expert.

"Combined with some [artificial intelligence], the AR glasses can really make our job a lot easier," one MRO engineer said. "I can now point my fingers to a place—for example, a lubricating oil cap—and it automatically recognizes the object or the key parts and tells me that it's open but should be closed. It also can show me, in a picture or a short video, how the object looked in normal condition or in its last service." When the task is done, engineers can sign off with their voice or even a gesture, if it's too noisy on the tarmac to use a voice command.

Rather than lug cumbersome manuals around or spend valuable time walking to an office to consult one, engineers can instantly access the information they need via the glasses. "I no longer have to go and look for the maintenance manual, which could take an hour walking back and forth. The manual is now coming to me, in front of my eyes!" one engineer told us. The AR glasses even make it possible for experts to advise mechanics on the tarmac in real time and supply them with pictures, videos, voice advice, and graphs.

The glasses also encourage more standardized performance. "It knows where I am in the process and points me to where I need to go next. Everybody is following the same process in the same order," explained another engineer.

## Welcome to the Augmented Operations

Wide-awake engineers, better compliance, a visual diary of the life of every component, and, ultimately, safer flights are all benefits of this single pilot project in the 850-aircraft airline. The AR glasses optimize performance not only by bringing more knowledge closer to the machinery but by keeping MRO eyes on the prize. Like most earlier forms of digitalization, CSA's experience suggests that augmented operations are less likely to supplant people than to increase their capabilities—a win for companies, employees, and travelers.

Today, CSA's first augmented operational system is still a work in progress, not so much in its ability to transfer data to or from the individual—although that presents challenges—as in adapting the technology to meet the capacities of human cognition. The AR smart glasses need to comply to the industry's safety standards, as well as meeting important objectives for privacy, comfort, display, connectivity, ergonomics, battery lifetime, noise reduction, multimedia interactivity, immersive experience combined with transparency, required infrastructure (5G, edge computing), and a knowledge graph that can provide deeper AI-enabled support.

## Only the Beginning

And that's just one application in one industry—imagine the many other ways the technology might be used. Already, thousands of companies around the world are experimenting with various aspects of AR technologies. And we believe this number will rise dramatically once we understand more about the best ways to manage the user interface on all those smart glasses, and the awareness of this new and highly adaptable technology grows. It's not unlike the moment when something called a website appeared on our desktops or, a decade later, when it became clear that apps were "the killer app" of the smart phone.

When the enterprise use of AR technologies has its own Netscape moment, we believe we will see the dawn of massive new opportunities in many industries. Airlines, for instance, will be able to understand their cost structure in much more detail than they do now, down to the part. Ultimately, this cognitive shift could change the balance of power within the airline business, away from sales and the front office toward the back office and the maintenance hangar (particularly as the carbon footprint becomes more integrated into the price).

And this is only the beginning. As the CSA project has demonstrated, virtualization has no limits. Any person or object in airline operations, from mechanics to the airplanes or the entire airport—can be virtualized, given enough data and enough modeling. By creating a virtual representation of a physical object, plus an ongoing stream of new information about its status, digital twins of physical objects and even people can give airlines unprecedented ability to see how something is performing *right now* and simulate or predict how it *might* perform in the future.

CSA's success suggests that AR is finally becoming part of our working reality. But there are still many unanswered questions. In our work for CSA, for instance, we have been posing many questions about how to bring the best out in people. When do people need reminders? What are the signs that their attention is starting to flag? What's the most efficient way for mechanics to communicate through their glasses to an expert, who can walk them through a complex repair? At the moment, the questions keep multiplying but, fortunately, so do the answers.

**TAKEAWAYS**

Thousands of companies globally are experimenting with augmented reality technologies. This number will rise dramatically once we understand more about the best ways to manage the user interface and the awareness of this new and highly adaptable technology grows.

✓ China Southern Airlines is one company that is weaving augmented reality, artificial intelligence, cloud computing, the internet of things, and 5G connectivity into a single network that is being used to extend human capacities, enhance safety, and improve performance.

✓ With AR becoming part of our working reality, there are still questions on the best ways to deploy it—but continuous experimentation is beginning to lead to answers.

*Adapted from content posted on hbr.org, April 5, 2022 (product #H06XJ7).*

## 7

# THE METAVERSE WILL ENHANCE— NOT REPLACE— COMPANIES' PHYSICAL LOCATIONS

by Vladislav Boutenko, Richard Florida, and Julia Jacobson

I f the combination of Covid-19 and remote work technologies like Zoom undercut the role of cities in economic life, what might an even more robust technology like the metaverse do? Will it finally be the big upheaval that obliterates the role of cities and density?

To paraphrase Airbnb CEO Brian Chesky: The place to be was Silicon Valley. It feels like now the place to be is the internet.[1]

The simple answer is no, and for a basic reason. Wave after wave of technological innovation—the telegraph, the streetcar, the telephone, the car, the airplane, the internet, and more—have brought predictions of the demise of physical location and the death of cities. Time and time again, such prognostications have been proven wrong. And while the pandemic *has* changed where and how people work, the trend of talented people, innovation, and economic activity becoming increasingly concentrated in fewer and larger superstar locations has consistently proven durable. Cities aren't going anywhere.

Still, the metaverse *feels* different. Its combination of technologies driven by virtual and augmented reality promises to make the virtual world a far more realistic substitute for the physical one. Recent remote work and virtual collaboration tools like Meta's Horizon Workrooms, Microsoft's Mesh, and Arthur are huge advances beyond Zoom and will enable workers to brainstorm, discuss, and interact with one another's avatars. They will create a much more realistic consumer experience for shopping for everything from fashion and luxury goods to art. It's easy to see why such an advanced technology might render cities and physical locations obsolete.

But the reality is that this metaverse, like each major previous wave of innovation before it, is less a substitute for location and more a complement to it. Even as the metaverse enables a far more realistic experience of the digital world and enables us to do many more things online—expanding access to rich content and wider pools of talent, lowering switching costs between locations and transaction costs in general, and vastly augmenting data-based decision-making and personalization—it will still be unable to replicate the emotional cues, body language, serendipity, and diversity that happen when human beings cluster and collaborate in real places.

The irony is that even as it stretches out the nature of location and enables workers and consumers to connect from just about anywhere, the metaverse is likely to reduce the set of places that truly matter. Only a relatively small number of large global cities have the size, scale, and connective infrastructure to function as global collaborative hubs. These superstar cities will continue to be the great clusters of innovation, global corporate headquarters, flagship locations for high-end brands, and the world's leading artistic, cultural, and research institutions.

The metaverse will make physical location a more—not less—important consideration for business. To some extent, this is already playing out: Cities like Dubai and

Shanghai are launching strategies aimed at attracting metaverse-focused businesses and people. For brands, this could mean ideal locations to experiment among enthusiastic early adopters. Companies will have to think more strategically than ever before about where to place offices and innovation hubs to attract and connect talent, where to locate retail shops to attract customers and heighten brand awareness, and more generally how to balance their physical and virtual footprints.

## The Metaverse and Cities Are Complements

In order to think strategically about the metaverse and location, it is important to understand the way the two complement each other. Here it's useful to think of both as channels—each good for transmitting different kinds of information.

The metaverse is a channel for delivering and using a lot of information in a convenient form. It builds on and is a step beyond previous digital channels like Zoom, email, messengers, chatrooms, and social networks. It will deliver video, sounds, pictures, text information, data, simulated videos, and avatars at tremendous bandwidth. A 2018 study estimated that 20 minutes in a virtual reality simulation allows some 2 million or so body language recordings.[2] This substantial and immersive virtual connection offers real advantages. Companies can collect richer data across broader networks than is possible in the physical world or existing digital channels. For many companies, this means new, cost-effective ways to improve their products, processes, and experiences. While some of this may involve virtual reality, it can also include more readily accessible modes like smartphone-enabled augmented reality.

While it is an improvement on what came before, the metaverse still will be insufficient to replace the fidelity of the physical world. It is the difference between experiencing a live performance and viewing one online. The physical world can deliver much deeper social, emotional, and sensory data—the ability to pick up on emotional cues or influence the room by modulating voice, moving around, and using body language. This kind of interaction remains necessary to build trust and social capital over time.

The metaverse is a mechanism for enhancing the physical world. A museum tour will be much more realistic supplemented by metaverse technology. A person shopping for a home will be able to take a much richer online tour of the property and the neighborhood before opting for a physical visit. Augmented reality glasses can add an overlay to a live event—live stats at a basketball game or viewer comments at a talk that's also being livestreamed. More to the point, a company might simulate and test a product digitally—a new shoe design, for instance—and tailor the final product according to social feedback before producing a physical version. Workers can engage online and prepare for their much richer on-site physical collaborations. In this way, the metaverse and physical spaces are better understood and acted on strategically in concert and together.

## Consumer Engagement Across the Virtual and Physical Worlds

A good example is customer engagement and the retail experience. A couple of decades ago, e-commerce revolutionized how businesses engage customers by adding a virtual channel alongside the physical one. The metaverse offers rich new opportunities for gathering data to improve consumer engagement and experiences. Companies like Meta, Microsoft, and Apple are building AR headsets that will enable consumers to engage in live events such as conferences, performances, and sports games as if they were physically there, with the additional overlay of digital content, data, and messages. Metaverse-enabled technologies could drive the next wave of personalization.

And, indeed, companies are already trying out new ways to enrich the customer experience through things like metaverse games with NFT rewards, exclusive drops and experiences to reward loyal "real-world" customers, and digital twins of physical goods. So far, companies have dipped their proverbial toes in the water here by porting the real world into the digital one—for example, virtual burritos, *Wendyverses*, and re-creating urban districts virtually in places like Decentraland. These are fun, but to date they offer little promise of replacing the rich experience of the physical world.

Such metaverse-enabled technologies would be a sizable improvement over what is available today, but still no replacement for seeing, feeling, or experiencing products and services in the real world. Consumer spending—especially among millennials—continues to shift from products toward experiences, and the enduring lesson from pervasive Zoom fatigue is that screens do not satisfy our desire to interact in person. This is what cities are particularly good at providing. In doing so, they provide platforms for using digital and physical channels as complements that reinforce each other.

Companies, including digital-native ones, have often used physical stores in key urban hubs—whether through permanent locations or temporary pop-ups during peak times—as complements to their digital strategies. Glossier uses its physical retail spaces to engage consumers and promote its brand with a highly Instagram-friendly store design, uniting its physical and digital channels. Nordstrom's Local model uses small-scale, service-oriented physical locations to augment its e-commerce offerings in key urban hubs like New York City and Los Angeles. Meta is opening a physical store to sell its AR/VR devices to access the metaverse. Instead of replacing actual stores, physical spaces can provide a way for customers to access the metaverse—maybe for the first time—and experience the latest AR/VR technologies. Physical spaces and locations combine with metaverse technology to offer more opportunities to add value by enriching experiences.

## The Virtual and Physical Nature of Work

The metaverse also promises to change the way we work, enabling much richer technologies for online interaction and virtual collaboration. Again, a big improvement over today's remote work status quo, but also not a replacement for people coming together in physical space. A big signal here is that leading metaverse companies are not just maintaining but expanding their physical presence in leading cities, even as they invent and expand their own remote-work technologies. Meta and Google remain headquartered in Silicon Valley, and the preponderance of metaverse technology startups are located in the Bay Area. Google is planning a major new urban campus in downtown San Jose and has expanded its footprint in New York City. As Google put it in a 2021 statement: "Coming together in person to collaborate and build community is core to Google's culture, and it will be an important part of our future."[3]

That said, the metaverse has an important complementary role to play here, in broadening access to talent pools—filling specialized or fully remote roles, ensuring a diverse employee base, and allowing employers to connect with job candidates virtually before investing in meeting in person. It will also likely be an important piece in how companies handle more mundane kinds of communication while socialization and connectivity happen in person. As this occurs, companies will likely need to review their social contract with employees, granting them greater freedom to choose where they live but doubling down on opportunities to promote cultural cohesion, mentorship, and learning, which are more difficult to do virtually. This new social contract may involve reinvesting savings from lower salaries for remote workers into programs that deliberately create such opportunities.

All of this means that companies need to think more strategically about what the office is for and where physical presence is required. While they can save money on real estate by letting go of some office space, companies will need a physical presence in key talent hubs and even better physical spaces for connectivity and collaboration. Offices in the era of the metaverse will be less focused on doing work and more focused on connecting and socializing—in other words, more café or canteen than cubicle. These urban spaces may even function as "portals" into the metaverse, offering employees the use of advanced virtual and augmented reality technologies in the office before they may be able to access them at home. The metaverse and the physical office, rather than opposing one another, will then increasingly work together to enable the future of knowledge work.

## Strategies for the Future

Put this all together and it means that the coming age of the metaverse is making location an increasingly central component of business success. To prepare for this, managers need to put location at the center of corporate strategy. Alongside their business and technology strategy for the metaverse, they need a complementary locational strategy. That locational strategy should be elevated to a C-suite-level priority and focus attention on the complementary benefits of virtual and physical spaces and locations. It should address questions around sourcing key talent locally and remotely; managing talent living in both "centers of life" and "centers of work"; and building a new social contract governing reciprocal expectations between the company and the employee. The strategy should assume the employee can work from multiple, high- and low-cost locations over the course of their career.

The metaverse presents a significant technological shift—bigger than just about anything that has come before it—that promises to make the virtual world far more like the physical one we are used to living, shopping, and working in. But it will not obviate the need for physical presence in cities. While the metaverse enables people, activities, and businesses to disperse geographically, cities will remain as crucial—perhaps even more so—as they are today to serve as hubs for in-person connection, engagement, collaboration, and innovation. Companies that meet people where they are and want to be—including smaller cities and towns—will gain access to a deeper talent pool and more satisfied employees, often at lower cost. But ultimately, the metaverse is likely to make leading superstar cities more important than ever, as this increasingly dispersed workforce will require places to come together and interact in the physical world.

Human beings are above all else social animals. We require one another and being together in the physical world. While the metaverse can effectively enable and expand access to certain aspects of work and consumption—from live events and experiences to digital art and avatar skins—it will never replace our basic need for face-to-face interaction and connection, even in a business setting. When all is said and done, the metaverse is not a replacement for physical location or cities. The two are much better understood, and acted upon, as complements to one another.

TAKEAWAYS

The evolution of the digital world should be seen as a complement to the physical world. Companies should develop their location strategies to maximize the potential of both the megacities that have become centers of talent and innovation and the new opportunities presented by the metaverse.

✓ In developing this strategy, companies should think of the physical world and the metaverse as channels, both of which are effective at communicating different kinds of information.

✓ The real world is good for creating emotional connection, while the metaverse is better at transmitting huge amounts of information.

✓ Companies should tailor their consumer and office strategies to utilize the strengths of both channels.

## NOTES

1. Brian Chesky (@bchesky), Twitter, January 10, 2022, https://twitter.com/bchesky/status/1480666399894736898?lang=en.

2. Jeremy Bailenson, "Protecting Nonverbal Data Tracked in Virtual Reality," *JAMA Pediatrics* 172, no. 10 (2018): 905–906.

3. Sundar Pichai, "Investing in America in 2021," Google blog, March 18, 2021, https://blog.google/inside-google/company-announcements/investing-america-2021/.

*Adapted from content posted on hbr.org, August 16, 2022 (product #H076U6).*

## 8

# DEHUMANIZATION IS A FEATURE OF GIG WORK, NOT A BUG

by Eric M. Anicich

O f course Friskies Shreds wet cat food was on the bottom shelf of the last aisle I checked. It was just that kind of day. As I crouched into a kneeling position to inspect the inventory, I scanned the customer's order glowing back at me on my smartphone: "Any seafood shreds with and without cheese. Twenty cans variety of flavors." But doesn't "variety of flavors" contradict the more specific request for "seafood shreds with and without cheese"? Or maybe the seafood category includes multiple flavors? Am I overthinking this?

As a business school professor—and, importantly, not a cat owner—my experience that day was atypical. As a driver for Postmates, however, it was just one of the 238 deliveries that I completed for the popular food delivery platform as part of an 18-month immersive research project to better understand the strategies that drivers use to craft a meaningful work identity. During my time as a Postmate, I drove for 130 hours, interviewed other drivers who had collectively completed 170,000 rides and deliveries on similar platforms (Uber, Lyft, DoorDash, Grubhub, Instacart, etc.), attended in-person and virtual company meetings, and reviewed and contributed to driver forums on Facebook, Reddit, and other websites.

In one sense, my recently published findings are not surprising.[1] Like many app workers in the on-demand economy, I too had customers berate me for not having a clairvoyant understanding of their apartment building's layout, parking restrictions, or door access codes. I too barely managed to earn more than minimum wage, despite selectively driving in some of the most lucrative markets in the country and using the most effective strategies I knew (such as resisting the urge to chase the notoriously quick-to-cool "hot spots" across town, avoiding neighborhoods with too many maze-like apartment buildings, and prioritizing multiple deliveries in one transaction over single orders).

However, my findings also point to something deeper and perhaps more concerning about the changing nature of work and our relationship to it that transcends app work in the on-demand economy. What I observed and experienced was a system that suppresses workers' uniqueness, experiences, and future aspirations. It was a system that treated people like lines of code to be deployed instead of humans to be developed. This is problematic because work is not simply the translation of physical and intellectual effort into money. What we do on a daily basis for work is part of our broader life narrative that makes us who we are.

Historically, organizations have played a crucial role in defining these evolving stories for employees by providing them with the physical, social, and psychological space needed to process and cope with confusing, disturbing, or anxiety-provoking work situations. For example, traditional organizations offer their employees the appropriate setting and resources to receive or provide advice, encouragement, feedback, and training; to help a colleague solve a problem or work through a negative outcome; to cultivate social connections through a secure and predictable network of coworkers, supervisors, and mentors. Collectively, these features of traditional organizations help employees answer the question "Who am I?" in the context of their work.

Many drivers in the on-demand economy, I found, struggled to answer this question. One driver I interviewed explained, "I try to bring my personality, but the app itself doesn't really offer that . . . the app sets the precedent to dehumanize . . . if you don't try to inject your personality, it just washes it out . . . I feel like a robot by the end of the day." A different driver put it more bluntly: "The driver is invisible [to customers] . . . the driver doesn't exist . . . it's like you're not really there."

It was not until I drove for more than 40 hours in one week in Las Vegas that I finally *felt* this reality myself. As I wrote in my research paper, what I experienced, and what many of the drivers I interviewed described, was akin to laboring on a stationary bicycle that is literally suspended, unable to gain traction on the path, any path, below—pedaling frantically, yet futilely; technically untethered, yet uninspired; at once dynamic and static.

This contrasts sharply with the messaging that platforms use to attract drivers: You can "move forward without limits" (Grubhub) as you "drive toward what matters" (Lyft). "From aspirations to relationships" (Grubhub) "no matter what your goal is" (Amazon Flex), you can "achieve your . . . long-term dreams" (DoorDash) because "you move the world" (Uber). At the end of the day, "you're the boss!" (Waitr). Yet these possibilities felt elusive, if not insulting to drivers, many of whom felt "stuck in the cycle [of driving] . . . going nowhere, and this is month after month after month," as one driver explained to me.

Frustrated by the platforms' unfulfilled promises, many drivers described exploiting a fundamental irony of on-demand work: The same characteristics that drivers experienced as threatening and depersonalizing (exposure to algorithmic management, no access to coworkers, few legal protections) also reduced personal accountability concerns. "You are in a car, in a private setting . . . you will never see that person again, you have no obligation to them," said one driver. Another driver added: "If you're in the corporate world and you are sitting with your boss . . . you need to be careful what you're saying and how you're reacting. . . . But in driving . . . if I say I like blue, and you don't like blue, I don't care, you know . . . because my manager is not going to look at me."

Outside the scrutiny of coworkers, supervisors, and repeat customers, some drivers successfully clung to unchecked fantasies about a more desirable future. ("Every day you meet many people [while driving], one of them can change your life!") Others rationalized away the more common negative experiences they encountered while driving (one driver claimed to have "a pretty good track record" having "only had one barfer and one person urinate in my car"). In addition to internally shaping, if not distorting their experiences, many drivers retreated to private online driver groups on Facebook and other platforms to exchange stories about the good and the bad, the absurd and the hilarious—seeking to negotiate their personal narratives by connecting with and comparing themselves to other drivers. These identity management tactics provided drivers with just enough psychological relief to continue driving.

When I decided to end my voluntary immersion in the driver community, I could not shake the feeling that the depersonalization of app workers is a feature, not a bug, of an economic model born of and emboldened by transformations that are underway across the global economy. This includes increasingly prevalent work arrangements characterized by weak employer-worker relations (independent contracting), strong reliance on technology (algorithmic management, platform-mediated communication), and social isolation (no coworkers and limited customer interactions).

Importantly, the effects of these transformations reach far beyond the type of low-wage gig workers that I studied; freelancers more broadly face similar existential questions and challenges.[2] With the coronation of agile workforces and customer-first philosophies nearly complete, the psychological contract—the unwritten expectations and obligations between workers and organizations—is at risk of being rewritten before our eyes. Indeed, the three C's underlying strong psychological contracts—a career that offers personal growth and upward mobility, a community that fosters social connections and belongingness, and a cause that infuses one's work with meaning and purpose—are all but absent for independent workers of all stripes.

At the core of the issue are changing preferences and practices with respect to "renting" instead of "buying" talent to meet organizational objectives. For example, a survey of C-suite executives and senior managers revealed that more than 90% think that leveraging digital freelancing marketplaces is either "very important" or "somewhat important" and more than 50% reported that their expected use of digital talent platforms in the future "will increase significantly."[3]

From this perspective, the 40 million Americans who have rented out their services to technology platforms like Uber, Lyft, and DoorDash may be canaries in the coal mine of the new world of work. What they experience today, millions more are likely to experience in some form in the future.

Of course, there are no easy solutions to these issues; many are existential and will require a reckoning involving values and priorities at the societal level. In the meantime, familiar ways of becoming and expressing oneself at work may no longer hold. As forces continue to erode traditional forms of identity support, meaningful self-definition at work will increasingly rely on how we collectively use and misuse innovative technologies and business models.

For example, how can companies deploy algorithmic management in a way that doesn't threaten and depersonalize workers? How can focusing on the narratives that underlie and animate identities help workers reimagine what they really want and deserve out of a career coming out of the pandemic and the Great Resignation? Will increasingly immersive and realistic digital environments like the metaverse function as identity playgrounds for workers in the future? How will Web3 broadly, and the emergence of novel forms of organizing specifically (e.g., decentralized autonomous organizations or DAOs), affect the careers, connections, and causes that are so important to workers? What role can social media platforms, online discussion forums, and other types of virtual water coolers play in helping independent workers craft and sustain a desirable work identity? In short, how can we retain the human element in the face of increasingly shrewd resource management tactics?

Now is the time for us to earnestly engage with these questions—from those who design, lead, and regulate these technologies and business models (software engineers, CEOs, and politicians, respectively) to those who study, teach, and help others cope with the implications of them (researchers, educators, and clinical psychologists, respectively).

Hanging in the balance is the well-being of independent workers the world over, many of whom are struggling to answer the question "Who am I?" in the context of their work.

**TAKEAWAYS**

Work arrangements in the gig economy are typically characterized by weak employer-worker relations, strong reliance on technology, and social isolation. What these gig workers experience today may be harbingers of what many millions more will experience in the future. Now is the time for those who design, lead, and regulate these technologies to engage with difficult questions about gig work and how technology will shape the future of work.

✓ What does an increase in gig, freelance, and contract work mean for the identities of people doing those jobs?

✓ Can companies deploy algorithmic management in a way that doesn't threaten and depersonalize workers?

✓ Will increasingly immersive and realistic digital environments like the metaverse function as identity playgrounds for workers?

✓ How will Web3 affect the careers, connections, and causes that are so important to workers?

## NOTES

1. Eric M. Anicich, "Flexing and Floundering in the On-Demand Economy: Narrative Identity Construction Under Algorithmic Management," *Organizational Behavior and Human Decision Processes* 169 (2022), https://doi.org/10.1016/j.obhdp.2022.104138.

2. Gianpiero Petriglieri, Susan J. Ashford, and Amy Wrzesniewski, "Agony and Ecstasy in the Gig Economy: Cultivating Holding Environments for Precarious and Personalized Work Identities," *Administrative Science Quarterly* 64, no. 1 (2018), https://doi.org/10.1177/0001839218759646.

3. Joseph B. Fuller et al., "Building the On-Demand Workforce," Harvard Business School, https://www.hbs.edu/managing -the-future-of-work/Documents/Building_The_On_Demand _Workforce.pdf.

*Adapted from content posted on hbr.org, June 23, 2022 (product #H073T8).*

# 9

# A PLATFORM APPROACH TO SPACE EXPLORATION

by Atif Ansar and Bent Flyvbjerg

The traditional approach to space exploration is to treat each project, meaning each rocket launch, as a one-off customized megaproject. NASA provides the classic example of this approach. It treats each launch as a big, bespoke investment—trying to deliver a "quantum leap" or "big bang." Donna Shirley, a manager on NASA's Pathfinder mission, describes them as "magnificent mission[s] in the grand old style."[1]

The problem with that approach is that the various missions are constructed independently from each other. Components and systems are not updated and transferred from one project to the next—they are instead reimagined.

The result is illustrated by the Mars Observer mission, launched in September 1992. With a 17-year planning and development cycle and a cost of over $1.3 billion in 2000 prices, it was slow to market and costly. On August 21, 1993, three days before the spacecraft was set to fire its main rocket engines and decelerate into orbit, flight controllers at NASA's Jet Propulsion Lab (JPL) lost contact with the spacecraft—the mission failed. That might happen with any project, of course, but it's sobering to reflect that even if the project had not failed, any follow-up would have cost as much and taken as long because NASA would have redesigned every component and system from scratch.

The new private space tech companies are taking a very different approach, treating rocket systems as platforms. They create components and technologies that can be reused and replicated, enabling them to start small and rapidly scale up. This is radically lowering costs, making space more accessible, and the demand is fueling plenty of investment dollars.[2] Let's see how they're doing this.

## How Platforms Work

Big tech giants such as Apple, Google, Amazon, and Microsoft are based on platforms. So are Airbnb, eBay, and Uber, whose multisided platforms have captured the imagination of investors: Airbnb does not own hotel rooms, eBay does not own warehouses, Uber does not own taxis, yet they facilitate interactions at scale among multiple sides (buyers and sellers). This has led some scholars to take a narrow definition of platforms, as capital-light digital systems that make markets.

But platforms aren't just a digital phenomenon. The terminology and industry applications of platforms emerged over the course of the 20th century, notably in the automobile and shipping industries. They are best thought of as a structured assembly of parts, subsystems, interfaces, and processes that are shared among a set of applications designed to create orderly interactions between multiple and potentially nonstandard elements and parties.

Consider containerized global shipping. Some of the elements interacting on a global shipping platform are interoperable 20- and 40-foot containers, cranes, vessels, communication satellites, and lighthouses; the parties include shipping lines, port operators, shippers, and regulators, among others. Whereas the containers are uniformly standard, vessels—despite many shared elements—are not. Yet the protocols of the global shipping platform enable orderly interactions, and shipping at a fraction of the cost pre-container.

The components of a platform are standardized as much as possible, as are the interfaces between components and users. This facilitates growth, as users and components can be added easily. As platforms grow, their functionalities increase (think smartphones that now host mobile banks, route maps, and streaming services as well as telephony and messaging services). As this process happens, they can evolve into huge and complex adaptive systems (or ecosystems, as some call them).

The outcomes are unmissable: Markets with platforms make services faster, better, cheaper, and more omnipresent. These forces, undoubtedly, cause disruption— platforms are not popular among those who find it hard to keep pace.

## How Is This Playing Out for Space Companies?

We'll focus here on just one company, SpaceX, but its competitors are sharing the same experience. The idea for the company was born when Elon Musk, then a newly minted billionaire with an interest in Mars, discovered that, despite spending billions of dollars annually over 30 years, NASA was nowhere near to landing humans on Mars. It couldn't even return astronauts to the Moon.

The problem, he suspected, was precisely that NASA treated each launch as a one-off event. Although they did learn a bit from each launch, they essentially started the next one with a clean sheet. They didn't reuse components, nor did they plan for such reusability. As he put it: "Throwing away multimillion-dollar rocket stages after every flight makes no more sense than chucking away a 747 after every flight."[3]

To Musk, reusability would be a key lever in generating commercial activity in the industry, since "the reason there is low demand for spaceflight is because it's ridiculously expensive . . . [and] the problem is that rockets are not reusable."[4] In 2021, SpaceX landed one of its reusable rockets for a 100th time. Reusability doesn't mean standing still—any more than Apple's operating system does. SpaceX systems and rockets undergo rapid iterative upgrades, which have expanded the overall capability set SpaceX offers its customers, just as Apple's operating upgrades do.

This platform approach to rocket-making creates a virtuous circle. Rocket systems made up of modular components are more easily upgradeable and reusable. This results in an increase in volume—in this case of launches. As people upgrade and recombine the components of their platform (the rocket) they can repurpose it, while continuing to scale. The variety creates the conditions for more scale, because it means that the platform has more value to more users.

In 2009, when its future was still in doubt, the company's only commercial launch took RazakSAT—a Malaysian Earth observation satellite weighing 180 kilograms—into orbit. In 2021, SpaceX set a record of 31 launches, with payloads of as much as 549,054 kilograms. Each launch now performs multiple functions: In June 2019, one of its Falcon Heavy rockets carried 24 different spacecraft toward three different types of orbit. The cargo included a privately funded solar sail experiment to harvest solar energy for interstellar flight, a NASA-designed miniaturized atomic clock for use in deep space, U.S. Pentagon–funded satellites to measure space radiation, and a container with the cremated remains of 152 people.

All told, SpaceX's 2022 launch revenues are expected to be around $2 billion for 40-plus launches, each of which costs one-tenth that of the typical NASA launch. Frequency is set to rise with ever lower costs and higher speed to market. Edgar Zapata, a life cycle analyst at NASA for 32 years, argues that 200-plus annual launches are within reach for SpaceX.

At its peak in 1964, NASA was launching into space at about the same frequency as SpaceX today, which is remarkable given the technology at the time. But that achievement came at an unsustainable cost of $40 billion in constant 2020 prices. By 1970, the budget had nearly halved, and by 1987 NASA's launch frequency had collapsed to a mere four per year. There was clearly no virtuous circle at play.

. . .

Companies like SpaceX have opened space up for commercial exploitation—and their platform model points the way to how mankind will solve its other challenges. In the context of the climate crisis and increasing levels of political uncertainty, how well we manage and adapt to challenges may well make the difference between survival and extinction. And if we do survive, it will almost certainly be because our solutions have been scalable platforms rather than conventionally planned megaprojects.

TAKEAWAYS

Private rocket companies like SpaceX have driven launch costs so far down that they have increased demand for services in space. The secret to their success is that they treat rocket systems as platforms.

✓ Platforms are often understood as capital-light digital systems such as Google, eBay, or Airbnb. In fact, they are best thought of as a shared structured assembly of parts, subsystems, interfaces, and processes.

✓ The traditional approach to space exploration—to treat each rocket launch as a one-off customized project—was slow and costly.

✓ Reusable components have made it easier to extend the functionality of rocket systems, enabling companies to benefit from constant incremental improvement.

✓ As humanity faces massive worldwide risks such as climate change, our ability to meet these challenges will depend on developing scalable platforms like these rather than conventionally planned megaprojects.

## NOTES

1. Alan MacCormack, "Mission to Mars (A)," Case 603-083 (Boston: Harvard Business School, 2003).

2. Matthew Weinzierl et al., "Your Company Needs a Space Strategy. Now," *Harvard Business Review*, November–December 2022, https://hbr.org/2022/11/your-company-needs-a-space-strategy-now.

3.  Matthew C. Weinzierl, Kylie Lucas, and Mehak Sarang, "SpaceX, Economies of Scale, and a Revolution in Space Access," Case 720-027 (Boston: Harvard Business School, 2021).

4.  Weinzierl, Lucas, and Sarang, "SpaceX."

*Adapted from content posted on hbr.org, November 11, 2022 (product #H07BZE).*

10

# DOES ELON MUSK HAVE A STRATEGY?

by Andy Wu and Goran Calic

During Elon Musk's dramatic, sometimes pugnacious, occasionally baffling campaign to acquire Twitter, we heard many of the same questions from both his followers and his critics. Why did he want to buy the company in the first place, and what was he planning to do with it? Will he make a lot of money, or will he lose all of it? Many questions simply boiled down to: "What is he thinking?!" Or, put another way, is Musk out there just winging this, or does he have a strategy? And if so, what is the Musk strategy?

We can all learn a lot—both good and bad—from Musk's other businesses: Tesla, SpaceX, Hyperloop, OpenAI, the

Boring Company, and Neuralink. Based on our research and teaching on strategy for innovation, technology, and growth, we see (some) method to the madness. Musk's strategy can be characterized by common themes across three areas: what fits into his *vision* for problems to solve, how he designs an *organization* as a solution to those problems, and why he can so effectively mobilize *resources* toward those solutions.

In understanding the strategy across his many businesses—and the significant risks of that strategy—executives can apply those lessons to launching and growing their own groundbreaking businesses. Investors can also use these ideas to make more thoughtful decisions when providing resources to entrepreneurs in nascent markets, such as Web3 and the metaverse. Finally, this framework gives us a lens to think about Musk's decision to buy Twitter in the context of his broader strategy.

## Vision

The most effective strategies often have a common trait: They build from a bold and clear vision of the future that gives the business a purpose today. In 1980, Bill Gates famously articulated a bold, clear vision for "a computer on every desk and in every home." Each Musk-affiliated company has its own sense of that boldness and clarity: Tesla's is "to accelerate the world's transition to sustainable energy" and SpaceX's is to "make humanity interplanetary." But to really understand Musk, we need to have a sense for the overall Musk vision that spans his many businesses as a whole.

## Problems, not solutions

While we conventionally think of a vision as being in pursuit of a specific type of *solution*, Musk seems to take a different approach: He pursues a specific type of *problem*. Specifically, he seems drawn to problems that involve navigating scale and overcoming complexity.

First, navigating scale means he selects problems that can only be solved through the commitment of massive fixed-cost investments. Consider Tesla's behemoth "gigafactories." The idea behind these factories is that mass producing electric vehicles at costs that make them viable for a broad commercial market requires massive scale. Giga Texas, the fifth Tesla gigafactory, is the largest factory in the world by floor area.

Second, overcoming a great deal of complexity—resolving dealing with multiple interdependent moving parts—requires the commitment of time and stamina for failure. Building reusable rockets, like Musk is focused on at SpaceX, is incredibly hard. For a rocket to be reusable, it must be able to slow from nearly 3,000 mph to a safe landing speed and nail a bulls-eye landing.

These types of problems have a clear potential for a sustainable competitive advantage—if you can solve the problem. A long stream of research by our colleagues and others suggests that a commitment to reaching critical scale and overcoming complexity can serve as a sustainable source of competitive advantage. But solving these problems is not for the faint of heart: It requires making "big bets," as our colleague David Yoffie documents in his extensive research about Elon Musk.[1]

## Problems as the solution

A vision dedicated to these high-scale and high-complexity problems provides several advantages.

Predictable road to performance. Even though solving high-scale problems is hard, performance and unit costs can predictably decrease as you increase production volume and build units over time—combined effects that are known as the "experience curve." (Moore's law, which states that computing power can double every two years, might be the best-known example of an experience curve.)

It's clear that Musk relies—at least implicitly—on the presumption that the experience curve will deliver. Musk wants to cut battery costs in half by massively ramping up battery manufacturing capacity himself, relying on technological economies of scale from improved production methods.

**Motivation for the long drive.** Pursuing solutions to big problems can be motivating for an organization, pushing employees to achieve wildly ambitious results. Still, there's a reason most people find them prohibitively intimidating. They seem so hard that it is not even worth starting or trying.

Musk is uniquely willing to go after these, and employees at his companies are well aware that they are trying to achieve seemingly impossible stretch goals. Musk famously asked Steve Davis, a SpaceX engineer, to build a part for the Falcon 1 rocket, which Davis estimated would cost $120,000, for $5,000. Davis eventually delivered the part for $3,900. Yet Musk maintains he makes achievable asks. "I certainly don't try to set impossible goals. I think impossible goals are demotivating," he's said.

## Problems as the problem

A vision grounded on combating high-scale, high-complexity problems brings about its own problems. Here, we'll focus on just two.

**Bumps in the road.** Most people are pretty bad at making accurate predictions. Humans extrapolate linearly, but complexity increases much faster than that. The result—as Wu's research with HBS doctoral student Aticus Peterson shows—is that entrepreneurs consistently struggle to set realistic timelines, particularly on complex projects.[2]

Musk, by his own admission, is no exception. Starlink, a satellite internet company operated by SpaceX, is still far short of Musk's 2015 predictions for where the company will be a decade later. As of March 2022, Starlink had just 0.625% of its subscriber and 1% of its revenue goal for 2025.[3] So far, the markets have given Musk an exceptional amount of leeway to survive being consistently inconsistent, but this kind of missed projection would spell doom for most managers.

**Running out of fuel.** The downside of pursuing a grand problem is that the road to a solution is long and the setbacks along the way are many. Burnout and disillusionment are real risks. A former production manager at Tesla said working 70 hours a week was not unusual and that getting fired from Tesla was the best thing that had happened to his marriage.[4] According to Ashlee Vance, Musk's biographer, a hiring manager would tell new SpaceX recruits, "If you want as hard as it gets, then great. If not, then you shouldn't come here."

Ultimately, the open question is whether Musk's organizations can sustain these types of working conditions over the many more years needed to reach the promised land.

## Organization

### Everything, by yourself

The most identifiable and consistent characteristic of the Musk strategy is how he organizes his businesses. Specifically, he engages in a strategy of *vertical integration* and *closed technology.*

Vertical integration. A firm that is vertically integrated directly owns and operates the various stages of a business value chain. SpaceX manufactures about 70% of their Falcon 9 rocket in-house.[5] In comparison, United Launch Alliance, which launches NASA spacecraft, only provides system integration and launch operations, relying on 1,200 subcontractors for all other operations. Tesla has an ambition to backward integrate into lithium mining. In contrast, traditional automotive OEMs rely on third parties in the marketplace to supply critical components.

Closed technology. A firm that has a *closed* technology strategy builds proprietary technology that is not interoperable with other firms. SpaceX's Starlink satellites use a highly proprietary technology that makes them effectively inoperable with other satellite dishes. Tesla's charging network in the United States is largely not interoperable with vehicles from other manufacturers. In contrast, an open strategy seeks to set a standard for the ecosystem by being interoperable with other firms. Nearly all the largest technology companies in the world rely on a more open strategy than Musk. For example, Google is working with HP, Acer, and Intel to launch fast pairing support between an Android phone and a Windows PC. The advantage of the open strategy is the potential for value-creating network effects that can lead to increasing returns and a winner-take-all market.

## Total control

These organizational choices have specific advantages that we can learn from.

Launching a new ecosystem. Bringing a new technology to market presents a chicken-or-egg problem: The product needs a supply of complementary offerings, but the suppliers and complementors don't exist yet, and no entrepreneur wants to throw their lot in with a technology that isn't on the market yet.

There are two ways of "solving" this problem. First, you can *time the market*, and wait until the ecosystem matures—though you risk waiting a long time. Second, you can *drive the market*, or supply all the necessary inputs and complements yourself. Consider the early days of electrification: It's hard to sell power turbines if there are no light bulbs and electric washing machines. Thus, in the early 20th-century, General Electric offered both generators and the products to use electricity.

With Tesla, Musk chose to drive the market (no pun intended) by supplying both the electric vehicles and charging stations that the vehicles depend on.

Capturing more value. By controlling the whole ecosystem, firms can capture excess value. Apple, for instance, can make extra profits by making its own proprietary charging cable, whereas companies that use the open USB standard cannot. Moreover, someone with several lightning cables in the drawer might find it convenient to keep buying Apple devices. Much like Apple, the proprietary charging adapters used by Tesla vehicles and charging stations (in the national network and at home) enable value capture down the road. Someone who has already installed a Tesla charging station at home might find it more convenient to stick with a Tesla vehicle on their next purchase.

## The risk of going solo

While we can justify Musk's strategy of doing everything in the short term, in the long term, this strategy sets him up for serious risks.

Missing out on the benefits of the market. By doing everything yourself, you run the risk of not being able to leverage the market when third parties eventually emerge that can offer inputs and complements at a better price or pioneer new innovations. While GE's broad offerings made sense in the early days, laundry machines and windmills don't need to be under the same roof anymore.

Intel suffers from this problem today. For decades, Intel maintained a vertically integrated strategy of doing both the designing and manufacturing of its processors. This strategy puts it in a bind today: When its manufacturing technology fell behind manufacturing specialist TSMC, Intel's chip designers were both technically and organizationally limited because they were stuck with Intel's in-house manufacturing capabilities.

Musk could run into similar issues. Should a new battery breakthrough come from outside the company, Tesla could incur significant unnecessary long-term costs because it would be stuck "buying" its own batteries.

Impairing network effects in the ecosystem. Technology firms face a fundamental trade-off between value creation in the long term and value capture in the short term: Choosing a proprietary approach inherently limits how third parties can contribute to the ecosystem. For instance, the Boring Company's planned 12-foot-wide tunnels are five feet narrower than the standard width used for city metros and thus incompatible with existing trains (although later pitches from the company included 21-foot tunnels).[6] If the company's own transit system works, it may lock in reliance on its tech. If it doesn't, there's no alternative use for the tunnels or machines and no outside assistance available.

## Resources

The only way to pursue high-scale, high-complexity problems with vertically integrated and closed organizational design is to have access to massive amounts of patient capital. And wow, does Musk have access to capital. Across eight of his companies, he has raised over $34 billion dollars. Neuralink alone has raised more than triple the amount of capital raised by Amazon.

This relationship between Musk and his investors is the core factor that enables his strategy. It's also the hardest to replicate. Most Wall Street analysts struggle to rationalize how it works, and most CEOs watch as markets cut Musk slack they could never get themselves.

How does he do it? To understand Musk's mastery of persuasion—and where the persuasion fails—we turn to Aristotle. Aristotle laid out three modes of persuasion: *ethos*, *pathos*, and *logos*.

## Ethos

Ethos is an appeal to the authority or honesty of the speaker. "He's got $13 million in." That's what employees of Musk's second startup, X.com (eventually PayPal), would tell recruits. He had invested most of the wealth he had made in the sale of his first company, and Musk has consistently had a lot at stake in his companies. His initial investment into SpaceX was $100 million of the $175.8 million earned from the sale of PayPal. He would continue to invest his entire personal wealth into SpaceX and Tesla until 2008, when he ran out of money and had to borrow from friends.

## Pathos

Pathos is an appeal to the audience's emotions. What Musk has achieved with his businesses is to develop an inspirational worldview, which Musk's biographer Vance describes as that of "a mad genius on the grandest quest anyone has ever concocted." Musk's showmanship gives him unorthodox abilities to marshal resources. Today, Elon Musk's tweets can arouse millions of retail investors.

One analyst recently noted of Musk's capacity to stir emotion, "Retail [investors] will follow Elon to the gates of hell and back."

## Logos

Logos is an appeal to logic, or at least the simulation of logic. This is where Musk's Wall Street critics might say he's weakest. Many of his businesses don't articulate a clear logic, which is demonstrated by the unpredictable way these businesses ultimately reach solutions or products. For instance, the initial motivation for SpaceX was to get people interested in space by growing the first plant on Mars. The idea was to modify a greenhouse that could be launched to Mars on a Russian rocket. No one in the aerospace industry believed he could get this done. Yet engineers and investors fascinated with his vision joined the company.

This example illustrates the logical ambiguity of his approach. Musk has spelled out some of his prior logic in a set of "Master Plans," but most of the logical basis for exactly how he will succeed remains ambiguous. But this isn't necessarily Musk's fault or due to any negligence per se: When pursuing new technologies, particularly ones that open up a new market, there is no one who can anticipate the full set of possibilities of what that technology will be able to do (and what it will not be able to do). Musk's investors tend to focus on the future and are motivated primarily by the appeal of Musk's authority and their own emotions toward him and their aspirations for the future. Fortunately for Musk, these are the kind of investors you want to have around when pursuing the problems his companies are trying to tackle.

## Twitter and Musk's Strategy?

Back to Musk's decision to buy Twitter. Did it make sense given the strategy outlined above?

"We wanted flying cars. Instead, we got 140 characters," Peter Thiel, PayPal cofounder and venture capitalist, famously quipped about Twitter in 2013. Musk has generally cast himself as more of a flying-car guy. What could he possibly want with Twitter? The thing is, over the last decade, the technological landscape has changed, and how and when to moderate speech has become a critical problem—and an existential problem for social media companies. In other words, moderating speech has looked more and more like the kind of big, complex strategic problem that captures Musk's interest.

That said, it's also a different kind of problem. For one, there's little evidence that the experience curve effects apply here. YouTube was founded 17 years ago. Reddit 16 years ago. Facebook employs more content reviewers than there are people working for SpaceX. These companies alone have poured tremendous money and time into an attempt to solve the content moderation problem.

Then there was the question of whether a reorganization along the lines of his other companies—taking everything in-house and making it proprietary—would work at Twitter. Most companies decide to insource AI moderation tools, which are scalable, and outsource human content moderation, because it's grueling and doesn't require technical skills. But vertically integrating mission-critical, nontechnical tasks at Musk's companies—such as welding at SpaceX—has led to improvement in both the task itself as well as adjacent processes. It's less clear how Musk's tendency toward closed systems, on the other hand, might capture extra value.

What is clear is that Musk's capacity to mobilize resources remains strong. He made a substantial personal investment in Twitter—about 10% of his net worth—reinforcing that he is aligned with investors and the long-term future of the business (*ethos*). On the other hand, Musk's appeal to emotion (*pathos*) has also been a bit complicated, generally polarizing people along ideological lines. Despite offering only vague plans and claiming that buying Twitter wouldn't be about making money (*logos*), at the time of his decision to buy Twitter, investors still seemed to defer to his record and his authority.

The saga offers another useful lesson: Many an investor has lost money by following inspirational leaders who ultimately failed to deliver and whose logic could never be, and never was, explained. In other words, the difference between genius and insanity is blurry and often unknowable until it is too late. What is clear is this: Musk has already achieved great things that no one thought were really possible, and he's done it through his own consistent, audacious strategy.

TAKEAWAYS

Does Elon Musk have a strategy? Or is he just winging it? Looking at Musk's many companies, projects, and initiatives, common themes stand out across three areas: what fits into his *vision* for problems to solve, how he designs an *organization* as a solution to those problems, and why he can so effectively mobilize *resources* toward those solutions.

✓ Musk seeks problems that require navigating scale and overcoming complexity.

- ✓ Organizationally, he favors vertical integration and closed systems.

- ✓ To finance his projects, he's able to marshal tremendous resources because he has large personal stakes in his companies and is able to stir public and investor emotions, even if the logic of how a given business will succeed may not be clear.

## NOTES

1. David Yoffie and Daniel Fisher, "Doubling Down: Elon Musk's Big Bets in 2022," Case 722-439 (Boston: Harvard Business School, 2022).

2. Aticus Peterson and Andy Wu, "Entrepreneurial Learning and Strategic Foresight," *Strategic Management Journal* 42, no. 13 (2021): 2357–2388.

3. John Koetsier, "Starlink Hits 250,000 Customers, Elon Musk Hints: SpaceX Booking Over $300 Million/Year," Forbes.com, February 14, 2022, https://www.forbes.com/sites/johnkoetsier /2022/02/14/starlink-hits-250000-customers-elon-musk-hints -spacex-booking-over-300-millionyear/?sh=123775287063.

4. Mark Matousek, "Ex-Tesla Employees Reveal the Worst Parts of Working at the Company," Insider, February 20, 2020, https:// www.businessinsider.com/ex-tesla-employees-reveal-the-worst -parts-of-working-there-2019-9.

5. "SpaceX—Low Cost to Access Space" (paper, Technology and Operations Management, Harvard Business School, December 9, 2015), https://d3.harvard.edu/platform-rctom/submission/spacex -low-cost-access-to-space/.

6. Sarah McBride, "Elon Musk's Boring Co. Pitches Double-Wide Tunnels," Bloomberg, June 18, 2021, https://www.bloomberg.com /news/articles/2021-06-18/elon-musk-s-boring-co-pitches-double -wide-tunnels; Carl Schwendeman, "Should the Boring Company Tunnels Be Five Feet Wider?" Inside EVs, July 10, 2019, https:// insideevs.com/news/358744/boring-company-tunnel-wider/.

*Adapted from content posted on hbr.org, July 15, 2022 (product #H075BN).*

# AI WITH A HUMAN FACE

by Mike Seymour, Dan Lovallo, Kai Riemer,
Alan R. Dennis, and Lingyao (Ivy) Yuan

All companies want to give their customers richer and more engaging experiences. That's one of the most effective ways to create and sustain competitive advantage. The challenge is to offer those experiences at scale without depersonalizing or commodifying them.

Throwing people at the problem becomes prohibitively expensive very quickly. And even if a company had enough employees to offer individual service at scale, in many situations customers prefer to interact with someone of their own gender, age, or ethnic background—an impossible staffing task. Moreover, research suggests that humans do not always produce the best results for every job. For example, Deloitte UK found that human-staffed contact centers are not only more expensive to run but often deliver a less consistent customer experience than automated channels—and they sometimes generate negative customer-service experiences.

Enter the digital human. Rapid progress in computer graphics, coupled with advances in artificial intelligence (AI), is now putting humanlike faces on chatbots and other computer-based interfaces. Digital humans mimic human communication as they offer a range of services: Companies are currently using them as sales assistants, corporate trainers, and social media influencers, for example. When deployed at scale, digital humans will radically change the business landscape. They may not be as capable or versatile as human employees, but they have clear advantages when it comes to cost, customizability, and scalability. Once "hired," they never tire, never complain, never seek a raise, and always follow company policy.

Digital humans are already making real money for their employers. Soul Machines, an autonomous animation software company, has upward of 50 digital humans deployed in organizations around the world. According to cofounder Mark Sagar, one client in the cosmetics industry, whose digital sales assistant recommends and models products and engages with customers about how to use them, has seen sales conversion rates increase dramatically. Visitors to the client's websites are now four and a half times more likely to complete the entire transaction and make a purchase than they were before digital sales assistants were employed.

For the past seven years we have been observing and researching the emerging field of digital humans, drawing on our decades of experience in the visual effects industry. We have worked alongside and consulted on projects with companies that create digital humans, including Pinscreen, Soul Machines, and Epic Games, witnessing firsthand the enormous growth and advances in the field. Within a decade, we believe, managers at most companies are likely to have a digital human as an assistant or an employee.

In this article we explain how different types of digital humans interact with customers and employees, discuss the situations in which using a digital human is appropriate, and present examples of digital employees working in organizations as diverse as accounting giant EY, Yahoo Japan, the Arab Banking Corporation, and the University of Southern California's Keck School of Medicine.

## What Is a Digital Human?

Meet Lil Miquela, a virtual online influencer with nearly 3 million followers on Instagram. The followers fully understand that she is not a real person—just as they know that Alexa and Siri are not "real." What they relate to is Lil Miquela's "authentic" and "genuine" personality, according to Isaac Bratzel, the chief design and innovation officer at Brud, the software media company that created Lil Miquela. Her personality is expressed through the products she endorses and the experiences she posts about.

Why do we ascribe a personality to what we know is an artificial construct? Because we can't help but respond instinctively to anything that appears to be human. Research from neuroscience shows that our minds are attuned to and react emotionally to facial signals. That's why most people prefer to communicate face-to-face rather than over the telephone. In the case of digital humans, we know that what we see on the screen is an artificial construct, but we still connect instinctively to it, and we do not have to be computer experts to interpret the facial signals and make the exchange work properly.

Digital humans are thus more likely to provide a meaningful experience than other automated channels, and customers are more likely to extend interactions with them beyond their initial search or transaction. Hao Li, cofounder and CEO of Pinscreen, a Los Angeles-based creator of digital humans, explains: "You want the customer to [explore] how things [like clothes] could be and how they might like them to look. From a user experience standpoint, you want to keep them engaged and able to explore the brand."

Fashion company ZOZOtown agrees. Now part of Yahoo Japan following a $3.7 billion acquisition in 2019, ZOZOtown controls about 50% of the market for mid- to high-end fashion e-commerce in Japan. With Pinscreen's help, ZOZOtown has deployed a group of remarkably lifelike digital humans to model fashion online and aid in customer fittings.

Another early adopter is EY, which creates digital-human doubles of its partners for use in video clips. The technology's translation function lets users make versions of presentations in multiple languages, regardless of whether the presenter speaks them or not. Advertising and communications company WPP has used the technology to send out internal corporate videos in different languages, all made without cameras. Victor Riparbelli, cofounder and CEO of Synthesia, the company that creates digital humans for EY and WPP, says that his firm's platform generates more than 3,000 videos for enterprise customers every day. "It is transformational to enable anyone in the company to produce uniform, on-brand video content for everything from internal training to personalized sales prospecting," he says.

Companies can create their own simple digital humans for a range of purposes—to make video clips, for instance—by subscribing to or buying licenses from Synthesia or other platform vendors. Users choose a digital human from a gallery of options and apply a simple text script or incorporate it into automated digital channels. If a fully interactive, intelligent digital human is required, firms will most likely need to partner with a specialist.

## When Should You Deploy Digital Humans?

Digital humans are not appropriate for every application. When customers seek a quick transaction, they are likely to prefer traditional user interfaces, chatbots, and voice-only assistants such as Siri or Alexa. But digital humans can be a much better choice when it comes to communicating complex instructions or describing features of a product. This is why YouTube instruction videos—rather than pages of text—are so successful. Someone searching for clothes online might welcome seeing the outfit on someone who looks like them to get a feel for how the items go together and whether the look reflects who they are. In such cases a digital human will engage the customer more, help complete the sale, and reduce the likelihood of product returns.

These questions will help you determine if a digital human is a good fit for the job you have in mind:

1. **Does the interaction involve emotional engagement?** A humanlike face will better address emotional aspects of an interaction, such as providing reassurance or empathy.

2. **Are users unsure of exactly what they want from the interaction?** If customers need specific information, then normally they are keen to see the details in written form so that they can quickly digest them. But if they are unsure, scanning pages of text is painful and time-consuming, and they often prefer to be able to ask for help.

3. **Is there scope to explore options and consider different approaches or outcomes?** Unlike straightforward online transactions such as buying groceries or booking a movie ticket, interactions such as shopping for clothes or working with a career coach have open-ended trajectories involving give-and-take. When

FIGURE 11-1

## Is a digital human the right choice?

*This flowchart helps you identify whether outcomes from a given interaction would be improved by deploying a digital human.*

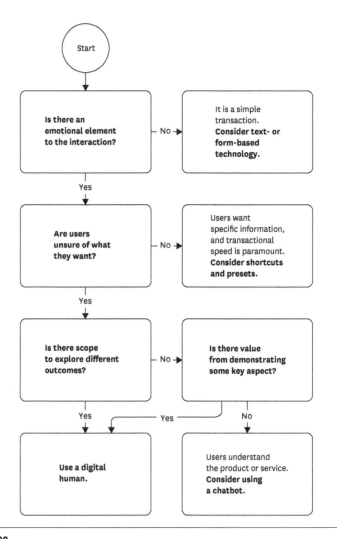

speed isn't the primary requirement, consumers often like to linger and explore.

4. **Could the user benefit from a personalized explanation of a product or service?** Is there value in demonstrating some key aspect?

If the answer is yes to three or more questions, it is worth exploring a digital-human option; if they are all true, it most definitely is.

## What Kind of Digital Human Is Best for You?

If the conditions are appropriate for deploying a digital human, the next step is to figure out what kind of digital human to design. First, consider the purpose of the interaction: Is the primary goal to complete a task or to engage in an experience? In many use cases, customers want to accomplish a task with measurable outcomes. Examples include booking airline tickets, filing a complaint, and retrieving order information. In others, customers want to engage with the company in some way—for example, by browsing through an online store, enjoying entertainment, or having a therapy session.

Second, consider the depth of the interaction: Is it personalized to each customer? In some cases, a person has

FIGURE 11-2

## Four types of digital humans

*Digital humans come in four basic categories, depending on the focus and depth of the interaction they are to be deployed for.*

Ongoing personal relationship

|  | Task-focused | Experience-focused |
|---|---|---|
| | **Virtual assistant**<br>Rehabilitation therapist<br>Personal assistant<br>Career coach | **Virtual companion**<br>Aged-care companion |
| | **Virtual agent**<br>Digital patient<br>Call center agent<br>Digital instructor<br>Sales agent | **Virtual influencer**<br>Social influencer |

Intermittent business relationship

regular exchanges with the same digital human, which "learns" and "remembers" the customer and becomes more and more personalized over time. In other cases, regardless of whether the interaction is transactional in nature or experiential, no personal relationship is developed between a specific customer and a specific digital human.

Mapping these two factors on a 2 x 2 matrix produces four categories of digital humans.

## Virtual agent

A virtual agent serves multiple users and does not develop a personal relationship with them. The agent's role is to complete specific, onetime tasks. For companies already using chatbots, virtual customer-service agents may be the logical next step. They have all the advantages of chatbots and amplify them through their realistic humanlike appearance. They can respond in any language and can tailor their appearance to the background or ethnicity of each customer.

Companies are also using digital instructors to engage employees in various types of training. Synthesia provides organizations with platforms for generating videos or professional presentations using noninteractive digital humans, obviating the need for actors, film crews, or expensive equipment. At U.S. international airports, for example, you may encounter a digital human giving instructions on how to clear security. Such videos can be developed directly from written text with text-to-speech tools. Victor Riparbelli sees real demand here: "If you are a warehouse worker and you get the choice between reading a five-page PDF manual or watching a two-minute video, it's a no-brainer. They don't care about how it was created." Not only are the videos less expensive and less time-consuming to create, he says, employees prefer the experience and remember more of the content.

A more sophisticated form of virtual agent is the digital patient, which the University of Southern California is researching for use in training the next generation of doctors and mental health professionals. Digital humans can simulate patients experiencing specific symptoms with a high degree of fidelity and realism. For example, they are capable of mimicking flushing, breathing responses, facial responses, slurred speech, and symptoms of PTSD or brain injury. Health-care organizations could hire actors instead, but that approach cannot easily be scaled up and quality is inconsistent. Digital patients also provide reliable measurements for training outcomes, such as which symptoms are recognized or missed.

## Virtual assistant

This type of digital human supports the user in completing specific tasks, and over time they develop a personal relationship. There are many types of virtual assistants: personal shoppers, home organizers, and physical therapists, to name a few.

Digital Domain, best known for creating digital characters for the Disney Marvel films, is developing digital assistants for Zoom, the video communications company. Its digital human Zoey, for example, attends Zoom meetings and monitors the conversation. Zoey can be cued to join the conversation by the phrase "Hey, Zoey" and deactivated by "Thank you, Zoey."

While activated, the assistant can answer questions and arrange schedules. Because Zoey has an active monitoring memory, she can associate comments and personal profiles with specific meeting attendees. Zoey can translate conversations into text documents and produce meeting summaries. She also analyzes the meeting content with natural language processing, especially sentiment analysis, and responds with appropriate facial expressions and micromovements, such as nods and eye glances, demonstrating her attentiveness and engagement.

Another example comes from a study of military veterans, which found that many people prefer to provide personal or sensitive information to a digital assistant. In the study, veterans wanted their doctors to know about problems they were experiencing but were reluctant to speak openly about their issues. They found that describing their symptoms to a digital-human assistant felt less intimidating and allowed them to communicate the information in a way that was more comfortable for them.

Digital humans are also often preferred in other contexts, such as education, human resource management, and dispute resolution. That's partly because they do not get angry, impatient, or distracted and can moderate their tone and speed of speech to match users' needs.

Of course, virtual assistants cannot replace humans for complex, nuanced interactions, such as explaining a serious illness or detecting mental health issues, because they lack any true understanding of what is being communicated. The digital human may question a person on a topic and react to a range of responses, but it never "thinks" in any real sense of the word.

## Virtual influencer

Virtual influencers supply their human followers with experiences, but they are not personalized. Everyone sees the same content on social media, for example. Although virtual influencers are carefully designed to appeal to specific user segments, any relationship a person might feel with them stems from that person's projection and not from any individual customization.

Virtual influencers operate in much the same way that human ones do. They share images of their experiences and post virtual photos of themselves having a great time somewhere wonderful in order to market a company's products. They have two key advantages over their human counterparts: They are much cheaper and require far less management. The people who follow them have no problem with the fact that the influencers aren't real because it is the experiences that they care about.

Virtual influencers have been especially successful in the fashion industry: Lil Miquela's carefully curated online presence has helped Brud achieve a valuation of more than $125 million prior to being acquired by Dapper Labs. ZOZOtown also deploys a range of virtual influencers to help market the company's products.

In the Middle East, Soul Machines has created a digital celebrity in Fatema, the public face of Bahrain-based Arab Banking Corporation. She was one of the first virtual, AI-enabled customer agents to humanize financial information. She talks to customers and responds, providing a humanlike presence. As a virtual influencer, Fatema is involved in Bank ABC's social media efforts and has a presence on Instagram aimed at helping customers feel more connected to the bank and learn about new offerings.

## Virtual companion

A virtual companion develops a deeply personal relationship with the user. Rather than focusing on completing tasks, the primary goal is simply to be with the user. Like a digital assistant, a virtual companion does not get frustrated or bored and has no competing demands on its time.

A promising application is in eldercare. Virtual companions enable older people to stay in their homes longer, which is known to be better for their physical and mental health. They are also much cheaper than assisted living or nursing homes. Digital humans not only provide companionship to stave off isolation, they also remind people to take their medication, facilitate communications, and alert medical professionals in case of emergency.

Similar opportunities exist in education. Children are more engaged when they watch other children. Thus a child-aged digital instructor could, at times, be a more effective tutor than a human adult teacher. The digital instructor could even be slightly older than the actual student—perhaps six months older—and shown to have mastered the subject, demonstrating that it is possible and serving as inspiration.

## Designing Digital Humans

In creating a digital human, firms must address two questions: Does it look right? And can it communicate appropriately with users in the given context?

## Appearance and sound

Appearance includes human features (such as nose shape and eye color), demographic characteristics (such as gender, age, and ethnicity), and taste (such as tattoos, makeup, accessories, and clothes). How the digital human sounds depends on its accent or dialect, vocabulary, tone of voice, and other factors. A great deal of design time is spent creating a "personality" for the digital human through appearance and sound.

The personality should fit the context. A user may feel more comfortable accepting medical advice from an older and wiser-looking digital human wearing a lab coat. However, that digital human would be ill-suited for a sales assistant role in the fashion industry. A smiling, perky digital human in customer service might annoy complainers. Conversely, a serious, mature digital human would hardly be a convincing virtual influencer for a hip lifestyle brand.

Brand image must be kept top of mind in designing digital humans, which serve as company ambassadors. Appearance and personality should reflect core company values and reinforce the brand image; mismatches may confuse customers or even damage the brand.

Digital humans must have a minimum level of human realism in the way they look and sound, otherwise they will be off-putting. But this is far less of a problem than it used to be. Rapid advancement in graphics technology and AI have dramatically improved standards. Tech that was once deployed only in Hollywood blockbusters is now available to most companies. Recent studies show that today's realistic digital humans are considered by customers to be more trustworthy and are more likely to instill a sense of affinity or trust than other visual forms such as visual chatbots and animated characters. While people don't require visual perfection, they want their virtual counterparts to be expressive and appealing, because what they're seeking is an authentic interaction—which brings us to the second design challenge.

## Communication

Soul Machines' Mark Sagar argues that for face-to-face interaction, the challenge is enabling digital humans to process multiple signals of intent and information. He has spent years working on how digital humans respond to and give verbal and nonverbal signals. "You've got to combine everything," he told us. "Speech-related gesturing, iconic gesturing, semantic gesturing, and all kinds of body language." Designers can't rely on scripted or branched prerecorded dialogues, because a conversation can head in any direction at any time. "Every time you add new dimensions that adds to the number of conversational combinations the digital human has to address."

Soul Machines uses advanced AI to circumvent this problem. The digital humans work from text and sentiment analysis and from camera input containing the human counterpart's emotional feedback, such as body language and facial expressions. Sagar is the first to admit that digital humans can never know a user's emotional state of mind; however, the more accurately they are able to analyze users, reflect their concerns, and apply machine-learning programs, the more meaningful they become to the customer.

Understanding nuances in human conversation can be challenging. Researchers at Digital Domain have made great advances in natural language understanding with their digital humans, but some things such as irony are still very hard to navigate. The problem is not just understanding and emotionally interpreting a person's comments; the AI engine also has to take into account previous interactions and the broader context of the situation. As impressive as the advances of the past few years have been in AI, companies must have a realistic understanding of the uses and limits of digital humans.

. . .

Digital humans are disrupting how firms engage with customers, suppliers, employees, and external stakeholders by offering personalized attention at scale. They are also being applied to internal corporate processes by transforming video production, training programs, and administrative support. And an emerging set of providers are creating, training, and supporting the deployment of many new types of digital humans. Firms that embrace this new technology will lower costs, increase revenues, and gain a sustainable first-mover advantage that slower adopters may find hard to overcome as customers become attached to their digital counterparts.

TAKEAWAYS

Rapid progress in computer graphics and AI is putting humanlike faces on chatbots and other computer-based interfaces. Digital humans now work in a range of roles such as sales assistant, corporate trainer, and social media influencer.

✓ When digital humans look and sound right—
and are able to communicate appropriately with
users—they are more likely to provide a meaningful experience than other automated channels.
Customers are more likely to extend interactions with them beyond their initial search or
transaction.

✓ For quick transactions, customers are likely to
prefer traditional user interfaces, chatbots, and
voice-only assistants. But digital humans can be a
much better choice when it comes to communicating complex instructions or describing product
features.

✓ Digital humans come in four basic categories,
depending on the focus and depth of the interaction they are to be deployed for: virtual agent,
virtual influencer, virtual assistant, and virtual
companion.

*Adapted from an article in* Harvard Business Review, *March–April 2023 (product #S23023).*

# About the Contributors

**ERIC M. ANICICH** is an assistant professor in the Management and Organization Department at the University of Southern California's Marshall School of Business. His research focuses on the forms and functions of social hierarchy within groups.

**ATIF ANSAR** is a senior fellow at Saïd Business School, University of Oxford, and program director of Oxford's Programme on Sustainable Megaprojects at the Smith School of Enterprise and the Environment, University of Oxford. He is a fellow by special election at Keble College, Oxford, and the cofounder of an AI startup, Foresight Works, that enables faster building projects.

**VLADISLAV BOUTENKO** is a managing director and senior partner with Boston Consulting Group's (BCG) Riyadh office. He leads BCG's business with cities globally and is a BCG Henderson Institute Fellow in the area of Future of Cities. His group's research focuses on cities' value proposition toward their residents, resident-centric planning of cities' physical and virtual real estate, the economics of virtual agglomerations, the role of technology in cities, and talent migration. Boutenko holds a MSEE summa cum laude from the Polytechnic Institute of Paris, Ecole Nationale Supérieure des Télécommunications, where he was a French government scholar.

GORAN CALIC is an associate professor of strategic management at McMaster University. Calic's research focuses on understanding why some individuals are more creative and some organizations are more innovative than others.

DAVID DE CREMER is the Dunton Family Dean of D'Amore-McKim School of Business and a professor of management at Northeastern University. Before moving to Northeastern University, he was the KPMG Chaired Professor of Management Studies at Cambridge University and a Provost Chaired Professor in management and organizations at NUS Business School, where he was also the founder and director of the Centre on AI Technology for Humankind. He is a Thinkers50 Radar Thought Leader, included in the top 2% of scientists worldwide, and a Top 30 Global Management Speaker. He is the author of *The AI-Savvy Leader* (Harvard Business Review Press, 2024). His website is www.daviddecremer.com.

**ALAN R. DENNIS** is a professor and the John T. Chambers Chair of Internet Systems at Indiana University's Kelley School of Business.

**JAD ESBER** is the cofounder of koodos, a New York–based Web3 company, and is affiliated with Harvard's Berkman Klein Center for Internet & Society and the New School's Institute for the Cooperative Digital Economy. He builds, writes, and speaks on the topic of social spaces and creative tools and the intersections with decentralized technologies. Previously, he worked at Google and YouTube, where he collaborated with and built for creators and artists in emerging markets. Follow him on Twitter @jad_ae.

**NITA A. FARAHANY** is the Robinson O. Everett Distinguished Professor of Law and Philosophy at Duke University; a scholar on the ethical, legal, and social implications of emerging technologies; and the author of *The Battle for Your Brain: Defending the Right to Think Freely in the Age of Neurotechnology.*

**RICHARD FLORIDA** is a university professor at the University of Toronto's Rotman School of Management and School of Cities and an academic adviser to BCG Henderson Institute.

**BENT FLYVBJERG** is the BT Professor and Chair of Major Programme Management Emeritus at the University of Oxford's Saïd Business School and the Villum Kann Rasmussen Professor and Chair at the IT University of Copenhagen.

**SUKETU GANDHI** is cohead of the global Strategic Operations Practice at Kearney.

**JULIA JACOBSON** is an ambassador to BCG Henderson Institute (BHI), where she works on the Future of Cities topic, and a project leader at BCG. Prior to BHI, Jacobson's work spanned consumer experience, omnichannel strategy, and the future of work. She received her BA in global affairs and international development, with a focus on urban development, at Yale.

**SCOTT DUKE KOMINERS** is the MBA Class of 1960 Associate Professor of Business Administration in the Entrepreneurial Management Unit at Harvard Business School and a faculty affiliate of the Harvard Department of Economics. He is also an a16z crypto research partner and advises a number of companies on marketplace and incentive design. Previously, he was a junior fellow at the Harvard Society of Fellows and the inaugural Saieh Family Fellow in Economics at the Becker Friedman Institute. Follow him on Twitter @skominers.

**TING LI** is a professor at the Rotterdam School of Management in the Netherlands and a visiting professor at Tsinghua University in China.

**DAN LOVALLO** is a professor of business strategy at the University of Sydney Business School and a senior adviser to McKinsey & Company.

**ETHAN MOLLICK** is an associate professor of management at the Wharton School of the University of Pennsylvania.

**KAI RIEMER** is a professor of information technology and organization at the University of Sydney.

**MIKE SEYMOUR** is a senior lecturer at the University of Sydney and a director of Motus Lab.

**BRENDA R. SHARTON** is a litigation partner and global chair of Dechert LLP's top-ranked privacy and cybersecurity practice. She is an internationally recognized expert, pioneer, and thought leader in the space. Sharton is Chambers ranked and a Legal 500 "Leading Lawyer" in Cyber

Law/Breach Response. In 2022, Sharton received Law360's MVP award in Cybersecurity and Privacy.

**JASON WANG** is the vice president of China Southern Technic at China Southern Airlines.

**ANDY WU** is an assistant professor in the Strategy Unit at Harvard Business School and a senior fellow at the Mack Institute for Innovation Management at the Wharton School of the University of Pennsylvania. He researches, teaches, and advises managers on innovation and growth strategy for technology ventures.

**FEI WU** is the CEO and founder of LLVision Technology.

**LINGYAO (IVY) YUAN** is an assistant professor at the Ivy College of Business at Iowa State University.

# Index